The

BIG WHITE BOOK

of

WEDDINGS

The

BIG WHITE BOOK

of

WEDDINGS

David Tutera

ST. MARTIN'S GRIFFIN

New York

www.stmartins.com

BOOK DESIGN BY AMANDA DEWEY

Library of Congress Cataloging-in-Publication Data

Tutera, David, 1966–
   The big white book of weddings : a how-to guide for the savvy, stylish
bride / David Tutera.—1st ed.
       p. cm.
   ISBN 978-0-312-56501-5
   1. Weddings.   2. Weddings—Planning.   I. Title.

   HQ745.T88 2010
   395.2'2—dc22

                                                    2009033864

First Edition: January 2010

10   9   8   7   6   5   4   3   2   1

To all my brides,
who deserve to be savvy and stylish every day

Contents

Acknowledgments

I gratefully acknowledge and thank:

- Sally Richardson, Elizabeth Beier, and Michelle Richter at St. Martin's Press: Thank you for your great enthusiasm for this project, for lending your editorial and literary talents, and for making the creation of this book such an enjoyable experience.
- Ryan Jurica: My angel, my partner, and my best friend. Thank you for always supporting every project I work on; your guidance and strength allow me to push forward and make each one a success. Together we make a great team!
- Liz Hart: Liz, you truly capture my voice on each page of this book. Your attention to detail in this project was so incredible. It is amazing how well we work together, and I can't imagine how this book would have happened without you.
- Eda Kalkay: My fabulous publicist, thank you for all of your hard work over the years . . . and for always being my loudest fan!

- Thank you to my staff at David Tutera, Inc., with special mention to Jaclyn Steudtner for embodying our savvy bride with her stylish illustrations.
- And my parents, Joe and Jo Ann Tutera: Thank you for showing me what weddings are truly meant to celebrate— the marriage of two people meant to love each other their whole lives long. You are my inspiration. I love you.

The

BIG WHITE BOOK

of

WEDDINGS

THE "OTHER" MAN
IN YOUR LIFE

You're engaged! *Congratulations!* Finally, you're en route to the day you have been waiting for *your entire life*—your wedding day.

I am thrilled your dreams have come true and that you have met the man who is lucky enough to walk your fabulous self down that aisle. My job, as the "other" man in your life, is now to help you get to Mr. Dream Come True with grace ... style ... charm ... sophistication. ... It is your time to shine in your two best lights: you being you (naturally!) and you being you in *love!*

I'm here to help you represent yourself in the best way you have ever looked, felt, and lived. (After all, you don't really think all the starlets in Hollywood do it without top advisers, stylists, and fashion gurus creating all the glamour backstage, do you?) Even the most magnificent of beauties need a little guidance from the pros. From this point forward, you will be nothing less than a beautiful, blushing bride-to-be, and you have me on your side until the "Just Married" sign on the back of your car is out of sight, off to destination Happily Ever After.

I have a personal love for (and strong devotion to) creating unforgettable weddings that are truly about the bride and groom. I believe weddings should tell the story of a couple, the story of you. Throwing a perfect, special wedding isn't about the grandeur of a palace ballroom or a couture gown: It's all in the details that touch the hearts of your guests and make your wedding day unlike anyone else's. Those details create your memories of a wedding that was unique and special, not just for you but for everyone who shared in your day. My job is to help you tell your story through your wedding plans and the execution of a flawless affair that represents you and your groom in the ways you want to share your love with your guests.

While that is *my* task at hand, your job is to prepare to look glamorous, get organized, and be thrilled about your wedding day! This book is designed to make you feel as ready and beautiful as you possibly can, inside and out. Through fashion, style, etiquette, poise, confidence, creativity, resourcefulness, wedding know-how, and—most important—*fun,* you are going to throw a spectacular wedding that will show off who you and your hubby-to-be are, and how the two of you are going to become as one in your amazing life together.

I created this guide to be an easy read that will provide all the fundamentals of planning any bride could need, from logistics and budget outlines that will help you get there in a financially savvy way (while I know your wedding is the end all/be all of parties, I do want to make sure you have something in the newlywed account so you can keep on celebrating your life in style!) to decor tips to make your day unforgettable. We will focus on your wedding, on you, and on all the things you need to accomplish on your way to "I do."

Throughout this book, I've created tip lists of "I Do's" and "I

Don'ts" to help guide you through the main planning process you will encounter as a bride. I have boiled down years of experience and hundreds of weddings and bridal clients to these fundamentals. To guide you to be early-educated brides in the wild wedding world, the "I Do's" and "I Don'ts" are here to help you avoid common pitfalls and unnecessary money expenditures, and to keep you ahead of the game. They're the main reason for this book (and probably the reason you picked it up). May you never have to say "I wish I had known then what I know now!" when it comes to your wedding. There are also "Tutera Tips" scattered throughout—fun ideas and valuable tidbits of information that I would tell you if you were sitting in my office and we were discussing each topic in person right now. Last, you will find sections called "Your Defining Moment," some quick glossaries of bridal terms that every bride should be familiar with when planning her wedding day. Mix these crash courses with your big dreams and you will be off to a great start already.

You may already have many ideas of what your dream day will entail. Perhaps they are things you've known you've wanted for your wedding since you were a little girl, or maybe they are new concepts you've noticed in one of the many bridal avenues of information. With all the input swirling around—bridal magazines, the World Wide Web, television, books, wedding merchandise, bridal consultants and wedding planners, suggestions from your mother, suggestions from your mother-*in-law*, suggestions from your bridesmaids, suggestions from your nosy neighbor/grandmother's bridge friends . . . a wedding can become a very frenzied state of affairs! So the point of this book and my goal for you is just this: I believe wedding planning should *never* be a chore or feel like "work." The planning duties ahead of you are not a series of tasks but a series of *experiences* you only get once; you should enjoy them to the fullest and share them with those you love and those who love you.

This is your no-pressure, humorous (but seriously useful) how-to guide, here to help you love every decision you make on your journey toward making the most important step of all: spending your life together with *the one*! The hard part is over—you found him! Now this is cause for a celebration: your wedding!

Among the abundance of wedding info you will be exposed to, *The Big White Book of Weddings* is your simple guide to staying focused, staying delighted to be a bride, and staying the course to self-discovery and finding the parts of yourself you want to include in your one and only day.

This book will lead you toward telling the story of you as a couple, and teach you how to share that story with your guests as you translate it into a celebration they will never forget.

So give stress a big kiss good-bye and save the drama for your dramatic entrance. After more than twenty years in the bridal biz, I've taken the best of what I know, and have broken it down to make it all easy to reference, from invitations to entertainment, from food to decor, from receptions to favors and quite a bit more.

Want to find out what cocktails to serve? Easy! Turn to the chapter "Eat, Drink, and Be Married!" and there you will find the most important literature on libations, some trendy tips, and some tasty tongue-ticklers under the section "Bottoms Up!" Is declaring your love on paper as difficult as drafting the Declaration? Tab to the chapter "You're Invited!" for invite ideas that uphold your right to be free from invitation anxiety.

Whether you are a princess bride, a chic fashionista, a lady of simple elegance, a destination diva headed for the waves, or a mix of everything, this book is for you. Grab a glass of bubbly, toast yourself as the beautiful bride you will be, kick up your feet, and, as you read, let me assure you that the only thing you will ever be overwhelmed with is joy.

I cannot be more delighted to be a part of your journey to wedded bliss, and I know you will find your way to sharing the best day of your life with your guests if you keep the one thought in mind that got you here in the first place: Your day is about celebrating love.

You're celebrating the love you have for each other, the love your families and friends have for you, and a love of life all around. I match *your* love with my adoration for seeing brides and grooms plan their perfect day with ease, and I can't wait to get started with you! Now let's celebrate your love with *style*!

—*David Tutera*

One

GETTING STARTED 101

The Planning Process: Think, Organize, Do (and Don't!)

He proposed!

This is a huge moment! Before we start on the details of your wedding, make sure you have taken time to *enjoy your engagement!* You will never get another chance to enjoy the rush and elation of being engaged more than once, so revel in the moment of being excited about your dream come true. I understand how exciting it can be, when nothing else matters or is on your mind except thoughts of how happy you are and questions of how you can ensure that your day will go perfectly once it's finally here. I once had a bride who was so thrilled about being engaged that she drove right off the road because she was so preoccupied by staring at her engagement ring. (Sound familiar? Don't be embarrassed. You're in love!) If you've taken the first key step of appreciating each and every moment of this process, you have set a great tone to starting to plan your wedding.

This is not a task list, this is an exciting list of experiences, each a celebration in itself!

This first chapter is about *preparing* yourself for the process: a crash course in planning. I am here to break it down for you in the easiest way possible so you can have both the wedding of your dreams *and* the wedding-planning *process* of your dreams!

The biggest mistake I see brides make is when they jump right into the details, the plans, and the purchasing before even pausing to think about the overall picture. It's like running a marathon without pacing yourself, and on top of that, it's like not stretching before you take off!

First, *think* about what you want to end up with in the end. Then *organize* those thoughts. Last, *do* exactly what you need to do to achieve your perfect wedding.

THINK ABOUT IT: BRAINSTORMING

I start with *all* my brides, even the celebrities, by sitting down with them to discuss what they want their entire wedding outcome to be. It's so important to take a moment for just you and your fiancé (no friends, no family, no coworkers or neighbors or celebrity influencers on your TV) to envision your perfect day. Write down all you have dreamed of or have seen that you remember wanting. Also write down things you like—colors, styles of music, eras of time, scenes in movies, and anything artistic that speaks to you. Dream big and get it all out there; this is your brainstorming list! The sky is the limit; even your wildest and least practical ideas can turn into inspiration down the line.

Ask yourself the most important question of all: What feeling do I want my guests to have when they leave? What emotions do I want them to take away with them? For example, if you answer with emotions like love, joy, faith, warmth, and serenity, this might help you discover you want an intimate, secluded celebration. If you want your guests to feel awe, excitement, and energy, this might guide you toward a lively party!

Throughout this book, you will find several of my lists of "I Do's" and "I Don'ts" regarding each topic. They'll look like this:

I DO's for Your Wedding Music

- Have a special song for your ceremony that creates the mood, sets the energy, and evokes your personality.

I DO's for Your Timeline

- Choose to have a unique timeline to change up things for your guests so it's not just another cookie-cutter wedding!

I DO's for Your Wedding Cake

- Have multiple layers of wedding cake flavors to provide options for your guests.

I DON'Ts for Your Wedding Music

- Just say no to hiring a band from your local pub that you just love hearing every Friday night.

I DON'Ts for Your Timeline

- Don't have a lineup of endless toasts scheduled in your wedding timeline. Keep your tidings of good health from becoming a speaking engagement by choosing various moments throughout your reception to highlight each speech.

I DON'Ts for Your Wedding Cake

- Don't choose a flavor for your cake that is inedible. No matter how many times your groom promises to take out the trash if you go with the "beer-batter" flavor because he'll be a hit among "the guys," pick something that is tasteful for everyone who will be enjoying it with you!

Having your own master list of "I Do's" and "I Don'ts" can help you stay focused in the long run. Reflect on the weddings you have been to, and think of what you've seen before that you both liked—and also what you promised yourself you would never do. You would be surprised what some brides end up doing that they said they would never fall victim to, either because they have been blinded by bridal bliss or because they are pressed for time and don't have an original brainstorming session (like the one you are so smartly doing right now) to rely on! When you feel as though you have a good collection of ideas and inspirations, it's time to start putting them in order and turning all these fantasies into realities!

GET YOUR PRIORITIES STRAIGHT: ABCS OF ORGANIZING

Now that you have your creative bridal juices flowing, organizing your ideas is the next step to making sure you don't lose any of them in the process. Create a binder to keep notes, all your great ideas, and, later on, your vendor contacts and contracts, timelines, and all your paperwork. Everything should be at your fingertips so you always feel in control. Organization will allow you the luxury of being calm, cool, and collected (literally!).

Organizing is not just about keeping files and folders: This step is also where you mentally organize yourself and prioritize all your ideas as you prepare to act upon them. Prioritizing is necessary to make sure that your wedding dreams, special moments, family tributes, and other traditions that will make your wedding yours don't get lost in the planning whirlwind. Prioritizing the fruits of your brainstorming session can be simplified into three categories: *non-negotiable, negotiable,* and *neutral.*

Non-negotiable is for things you will not change, no matter what. Example: You have always wanted a spectacular white cake of many, many layers with gardenias because they were your grandmother's favorite flower, and you promised her you would give her that special tribute.

That would go under non-negotiable! This is something you

would be truly upset by and that would potentially sadden you on your wedding day if you did not get it. (And no. You may not put everything under the sun under non-negotiable. You have to pick and choose your battles, sassy lady! . . . and *that's* a great lesson to learn about being married!) Only "must-haves" go here.

Negotiable is for things you want, but you are willing to forgo. Example: Perhaps you know you want live music, but you don't know if you can afford it and you are willing to give it up if you need to spend your money on more important things (like your special, multilayer gardenia-topped cake).

This would go under negotiable. It is something that you would like, but you realize you are impartial enough to it that it can go if it needs to. You would, in an ideal world, like to have these items, but you also realize there are options and you're willing to compromise.

Neutral is for things you do not have a stance on that you can prioritize at the bottom (and also delegate the responsibility to bridesmaids, moms, sisters, or friends to handle!). Example: Maybe you really don't mind what the flowers on the end of each ceremony pew look like, or what varietal of wine is served at your cocktail hour. You guessed it! These would go under neutral. These are things that you must choose for your wedding, but they are not as important as things that are non-negotiable, or negotiable. They are just items you need to make sure are included to complete your wedding.

Throughout this book (and in a very handy chart on my Web site, www.davidtutera.com), I've listed all the things in a wedding you may potentially have the opportunity to spend your money on. By no means do you need to purchase everything any wedding "expert" says you need to purchase to have the perfect wedding! If that were the case, all weddings would be more than a quarter of a million dollars (and if that's your budget, put this book down and call me so we can go out for a night on the town!). Highlight the items you definitely want to spend money on. Then rank those items in order of importance to you: 1, 2, 3, etc. Having trouble putting things in order? Look back on your "negotiating" list. You've already done the thinking!

If you're still having trouble, think of it all in terms of "this versus that." Is having a band more important to you than having lots and lots of flowers? Rank band above flowers. Is your money best allocated toward helping your bridesmaids afford the dresses you want versus getting an expensive veil? Bridesmaids over veil. As you prioritize, make notes. Later on, in the bridal whirlwind, if you want to remember why you made a certain choice, you'll know!

Once you have categorized what is important to you, you have laid the foundation for your entire wedding, and you have given yourself a solid idea of how to build your wedding and what you need to purchase—and, most important, you know what is important to you! You can go forward with a clear idea of your priorities as you prepare yourself to smartly spend!

DO YOUR HOMEWORK:
RESEARCHING BEFORE ACTING

The excitement of getting married can be misdirected into excitement to spend, spend, spend! Don't fall into "bridal bargain" shopping, especially with the Internet bridal Web sites that beckon you to purchase the votives with your initials on them . . . or disposable cameras in your colors for your tables . . . or the fake candles you "like better" than the votives with your initials on them that you found earlier, but you couldn't choose which to get, so you got both. . . . You're a smart, sensible, and stylish bride! As long as you do your homework and research before you act (or react!), you'll pass the test of being a brilliant bride with flying colors.

I advocate that your money is very valuable. (Don't you?) It should be spent only in the wisest of ways, so here's your study guide—your cheat sheet for when you do your homework on your vendors.

- Research vendors and everyone you are considering for hire. Work with vendors who are in business to take care of you! Sometimes the personality of a vendor can become very high maintenance, and you might find that you're spending more time making sure your vendor is happy than vice versa. Good vendors will always be happy to provide reference letters of past happy clients. Don't be afraid to ask! Take multiple meetings with multiple vendors to test out how you feel about each one and to see samples of their work. Last, speak to past clients (you can find them on bridal blogs and chats) to find out what they really thought.

- Work on your budget until you know *exactly* how much you can spend on your dress, accessories, flowers, favors, etc. (You don't have to carve these figures in stone, but you should know in the back of your head when you are about to buy something if it is within your means or not.)

- Get a good idea of how much things realistically cost. Save yourself from getting sticker shocked when you realize how quickly a wedding adds up—after you've already started spending. Be a well-educated bride and put the feelers out first. How much are flowers? How much do dresses run? How much can cakes be? Don't purchase anything before you understand how much your other elements—and the additions that come with them—will be. That sounds daunting, but do not fear, this leads us to our next section—being a budget-friendly bride!

- Plan out what details you need to buy. It's like going to the grocery store. When you go without a list, everything looks so appetizing that you end up in the checkout line with way more than what you need! When you plan your wedding, you need to do the same thing—make your list first.

I am so serious about not letting you waste your money that I want you to pledge to stay your brilliant, money-saving, savvy self right now. Make the commitment (I am your "other man," remember!) with yourself.

CONTRACT

I _____ (as a brilliant, money-saving, savvy bride) acknowledge that small purchases, just because they are small purchases, do not exempt them from leading up to big expenses.

I solemnly promise not to let my excitement get the best of me, leading me to purchase anything without checking it for both price and quality.

I vow not to purchase anything that only "kind of" goes with my theme, my colors, or my wedding in general. Such items include but are not limited to: seasonal oddities that have little to no relevance to my wedding date (i.e., cute sandals in my colors when my wedding is in November), decorations that go with a theme that is fun but is not mine (if I am having a beach wedding, I will not purchase anything that has to do with a princess wedding; I am not having a royal beach wedding), favors that are cheaply made (even though I am enticed by them because I get a lot of them), and/or anything that does not exist in nature (including turquoise "silk" rose petals, figurines of singing animals, or anything neon).

X _____

(the brilliant, money-saving, savvy bride)

The Fine Print: Stay true to yourself and to the wedding you envisioned for yourself in the beginning. Change and discovery are good along the way, as long as you stay focused and don't end up paying (literally and figuratively) for it later!

Two

THAT COSTS HOW MUCH? OR, MY DAD SO WON'T PAY THAT

The Bride's Guide to Savvy Spending and Budgeting

Money makes the world go 'round . . . and when you budget properly, you can *absolutely* prevent your number-crunching from spinning out of orbit.

My rule of thumb: There's no need to spend a ton of money to have an elegant wedding; you just have to spend the money you *do* have *wisely*!

The budget is the number-one place I see my brides go from wishful to woeful . . . and it's all because they don't create a good, solid strategy of how they are going to afford all the wonderful accoutrements of their wedding. The stress of finances (in addition to the wedding commotion) takes them into uncharted—and unpaid for—territory. How I wish they all knew this was preventable! You just have to be a well-educated bride—and now that you've "done your homework," you're ready to graduate to part two! Sounds like a perfect time for a few life lessons on bridal bucks, so let's hit the budget books, my lovely bride-to-be, and save you some cash for the honeymoon!

CREATE YOUR BUDGET BEFORE YOU SPEND A DIME

Before you make any financial commitments to anything (a dress, a caterer, even a venue), it's important to first plot out how you will pay for the wedding shebang as a whole. What good is it to have a gorgeous fancy wedding gown . . . and no reception to show it off at? ("All dressed up and nowhere to go" is *not* what we're going for!) Ensuring you have enough money to purchase what you want (and keeping you out of a disaster zone of debt to come home to from your honeymoon) is our priority here.

Tutera Tip: Don't forget that you don't have to buy a lot of things or have an abundance of trinkets to have a lavish, well-done wedding. Anyone on any budget can have a beautiful ceremony and reception. There is beauty in extravagance but there is also beauty in simplicity!

Each bride's budget is different. Instead of giving an exact dollar figure of how much should be spent on each element, here is an idea of the *percentages* of your budget that should be allotted.

The Budget Breakdown

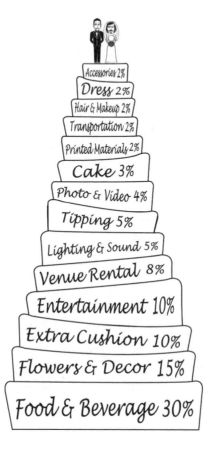

WHAT TO EXPECT (AND QUESTIONS TO ASK WHEN RESEARCHING COSTS)

Budgeting is a constant work in progress throughout the duration of the wedding-planning process. Many variables come into play that determine how much you have to spend in other areas, so it's a continuous bridal balancing act. To get you acquainted with what will be in your wedding equilibrium, here are some tips to keep you from toppling (in order of what the most expensive items, from highest to lowest, will traditionally be).

Food and Beverage Expenses

Food and beverage expenses, being the most costly (and most controlling) element of your budget, play a large role in your budget and will give you the best idea of what you will be left to work with monetarily.

When you decide how much your food per person will cost (or when you decide how much you can pay for food per person, whichever comes first), you can then determine the general cost of your wedding. A very simple equation can get you there:

YOUR GUEST COUNT: _____

×

COST PER PERSON FOR FOOD AND BEVERAGE EXPENSES (for both cocktails and reception): $ _____

+ TAX: $ _____

+ SERVICE CHARGE: $ _____

+ GRATUITY (separate from the service charge): $ _____

_____

YOUR FOOD AND BEVERAGE COST: $ _____

Is the number higher than you were expecting? Before you panic, remember that food and beverage will be your highest cost (and this is the category that makes a wedding costly from the get-go). Also know that there are ways to cut that number down, which I explain in the "Eat, Drink, and Be Married!" chapter.

Tutera Tip: Guarantee the lowest guest count possible. You can always go up from there, and you won't ever be contractually obligated to pay for more people than you can guarantee.

Tutera Tip: Tax and tip amounts (often referred to by caterers as your amount per person followed by a "plus plus") are important to remember, especially when dealing with large numbers. "Tax" may have the connotation of being just a few dollars here or there on an item of clothing or a slushy from the convenience store, but when you're dealing with large numbers, it can be a pretty big chunk of change that you need to actually budget for. In your contract, you will find a line item for tax and service charge, and often a blank line for additional gratuity that you will determine yourself. ("Service charges" go to the establishment to pay for the actual labor wages, so that "additional gratuity" is the tip for your servers, captains, and maître d'.) Don't assume anything is included if it's not listed: Look for any hidden fees and ask if there are any charges you haven't seen yet. Is there a charge for rentals or for using or traveling to your venue? What about coat check or valet? It may be a lot of question asking, but better safe than sorry! It's your right to know what you will be paying for. Protect yourself when it comes to your signature and your money.

SMARTLY SPEND, SMARTLY SAVE

- Beverages are the fastest route to send your budget through the reception hall roof. Ask about special packages. Inquire about the difference in price and quality between a "premium" bar and a "top-shelf" bar. Can you save money by bringing your own alcohol, and paying a corkage fee to do so?
- Ask for options: Do you need a four-course dinner or can you scale down to three? Do you need stations or can you save by having passed hors d'oeuvres? (While you're at it, ask what entrees and hors d'oeuvres are priced lower than others.)
- Do they include a wedding cake in their costs? (If it's optional, is it cheaper than hiring a bakery?)
- Often, catering companies will include basic linens, flatware,

glassware and china, tables and chairs, and table numbers and accessories. Some provide centerpieces and/or candles. Find out all the details of what's included in the price-per-person cost up front.

- Discuss any upgrades that are possible—don't wait to find out when you're too late and a dollar short (no joke!).
- Ask what your catering company may have in stock that you can rent (or have included), down to the color of linens to match the napkins and the ties of your servers.
- How many waiters are you getting? Ask about staffing, and what will be provided. The typical need is one waiter per every ten guests for regular service, and two waiters per every ten guests for formal service.

Flowers and Decor

Your major costs for flowers and decor can be broken down into three categories: Personal Flowers, Ceremony Flowers, and Reception Flowers. Here's a worksheet for you to "plug and chug" your numbers:

PERSONAL FLOWERS

YOUR BRIDAL BOUQUET: $ _____

YOUR TOSS BOUQUET: $ _____

MAID OF HONOR BOUQUET: $ _____

BRIDESMAID BOUQUETS: $ _____

× _____ (number of bridesmaids) = $ _____

JUNIOR BRIDESMAID BOUQUET: $ _____

FLOWER GIRL ACCESSORIES (crown, basket with petals): $ _____

CORSAGES FOR WOMEN (mothers, grandmothers): $ _____

BOUTONNIERES FOR MEN (groom, groomsmen, fathers, grandfathers,

ushers, ringbearer): $ _____

Decor

The cost for decor is based on your guest count and how many tables the guests will take up. With those numbers (or estimated numbers) you can figure out how many tables you will need to decorate.

HOW MANY TABLES YOU HAVE: _____

×

HOW MUCH YOUR CENTERPIECES WILL COST: $ _____

_____

BASE COST FOR RECEPTION FLORAL: $ _____

OPTIONAL FLORAL ADDITIONS

Aisle Decor	Escort Card Table
Cocktail Tables	Buffet Tables
Restrooms	Bar Arrangement
Foyers/Entrances	Stage Decor
Sweetheart Table	Cake Table Flowers

Lutera Tip: To cut costs from having to pay for large arrangements for each table, ask for a mix of high and low arrangements, or a variation of three correlating arrangement designs (varying in cost) mixed throughout the tables. This will get you out of paying for all large arrangements and will also add aesthetic variety to the look of your reception on many visual levels.

Ceremony Flowers

The amount of flowers (if any) needed for your ceremony is dependent on your ceremony location. Different venues require different floral uses, needs, and limitations. Once you choose your ceremony venue, determine where you would like to (and where you can afford to) add decor.

Tutera Tip: There is nothing wrong with a simple ceremony design—it is just one location! "I Do" like simplicity. Let the wedding service itself be the main attraction.

SMARTLY SPEND, SMARTLY SAVE

- Ask your florist if your ceremony flowers can be reused at the reception, simply by moving them over and repositioning them. There's no sense in paying for twice as many or not getting your money's worth out of them all night!
- See if, in a design you like, there are alternate, more cost-effective flowers that can be substituted to save you money. Are the types of flowers you want only available in a particular season? Instead, ask what flowers and colors are in season, and if they are less expensive.
- Ask your venues if you may borrow their decorations. Some churches, synagogues, or wedding ceremony venues stock decor, candleholders, or pew decorations for special occasions.
- Make sure your florist has discussed delivery (and pickup) of your flowers to and from your location, and any delivery fees.

Photographer/Videographer

A picture is worth a thousand words and video captures life in a way only video cameras can. When budgeting for your photographer and/or videographer, here are some money-saving ideas to keep cash in your pocket and the cameras rolling.

This is a vendor cost that's true to the phrase "What you put into it is what you get out of it." The more time and money you put into working with your photographer and videographers, the higher quality you will get in the end.

Some brides want both photos and a video—and hire someone to shoot each. If your budget does not allow for hiring two different specialists, there are companies that dabble in both photography and videography, and can offer you a package deal that includes both a photographer and a cameraman. Another way to save is to have your photographer put your wedding day photos into a video montage with music, which keeps you from having to hire a videographer. Last, you can choose to have just one or the other, whichever is more important to you! Either way, you will have great documentation of your beautiful day.

Know what is included in your options from the get-go. Know all charges and find out as much information as you can about the details of purchasing images, books, photo accessibility, special effects, sizing, editing, and ordering reprints years from now. As you're plotting out what you will need in your package, cover all your bases by counting all the people besides you and your groom who will "need" photographic items—an album for you and your groom, parents' books, any additional prints for family or friends (or you)—and ask what the cost is for each additional image in case, after the wedding, someone wants a particular shot.

Tutera Tip: Discuss every possible option up front instead of talking about it afterward. Make sure everything you need is in the package price. If you wait until after the wedding, you will spend much more on photos you can't resist if you didn't ask or budget for them in the beginning.

SMARTLY SPEND, SMARTLY SAVE
- What are the rates of the photographer's/videographer's services? Are there package deals?
- How many people will they send to capture your event?
- Is there an overtime cost?
- What does your package include?
- How much are photos after your wedding if you want to go back and purchase them?

Printed Materials

Your printed-materials cost will be a culmination of the materials themselves, plus postage. Your printed goods include save the dates, invitations, the Rsvp card and prestamped return envelope, a direction and accommodations card, calligraphy and your embellishments, escort and place cards, table and menu cards, programs, and any additional notes, stationery, or signage. Your postage costs are:

NUMBER OF SAVE THE DATES × POSTAGE STAMP COST (may vary due to size and weight)

+

NUMBER OF INVITATIONS × POSTAGE STAMP COST (may vary due to size and weight)

+

NUMBER OF REPLY CARD ENVELOPES (same number as invitations) × POSTAGE STAMP COST (may vary due to size and weight, especially for larger invitations)

_____

TOTAL POSTAGE COST: $ _____

SMARTLY SPEND, SMARTLY SAVE

- When you ask your invitation designer for a prototype of your invitation, is it no charge? If not, how much is it? If you are being charged per prototype, will the costs of each be applied to your overall bill?
- Heavy cardstock, multiple layers, and unique packaging will increase cost due to weight and postage. As you are budgeting, plan for the right amount of postage, or vice versa: Plan the look of your invitations around what you can budget. Don't decide on your final invitation until you know what the general cost will be for postage!

Music and Entertainment

Entertainment can be as affordable—or as extremely pricey—as you like! But you don't need to have a rock-star budget to have your entertainment be a hit with your guests.

Consider your entertainment options in three price-structured tiers:

Most Expensive—The Bandstand

A multipiece band or orchestra is the tried-and-true (and most luxurious) way to entertain your guests with sound. From horn sections to lead singers, backup singers and fancy apparel, a band can set the tone for a rockin' reception! Hiring a great big band is great big fun but also comes with a great big price tag. Paying for, let's say, a twelve-piece band could cost several hundreds of dollars per musician. If you have the budget and the desire—play on!

Tutera Tip: Make sure the band includes a sound system that they come and set up themselves in their contract: They have both the time and the power resources. Also, each band comes with a rider (a contract that details everything they require). Make sure you read every part of the rider to see what you are promising them before signing! Riders can also be negotiable at times, so work through the band's company to discuss your terms of agreement. Most riders include travel, food, water, clothing racks, a break room, and some staging requirements. Be careful, though—I once saw a rider that included free food and drinks for the performer's entourage of fifteen friends!

Tutera Tip: Be very aware of start times, end times, and overtime charges on your entertainment contracts. Overtime can bust the budget that you worked so hard on! Is overtime counted in thirty-minute increments or sixty-minute increments? (This is important to know when Uncle Earl is standing in the front

*yelling "Encore!") A wedding that ends with the dance floor full
is always better than going into overtime and ending up with a
dance floor of twenty guests out there alone. End on a high note
with no overtime and no extra charges.*

Moderately Expensive—Mixing It Up

There's something about live music that makes many brides gravitate toward it—the energy from the band that gets guests on their feet. If hiring a full band or orchestra is beyond your budget, there are alternatives that still keep that personal vibe going.

For instance, you can hire a DJ who also has a few instrumentalists who play with the music for a more robust, interactive sound. This is a great option to keep the familiar sound of favorite recorded songs and still have something special!

You also may consider hiring performers on a smaller scale: A single amplified guitarist can set the entire audible ambience at a ceremony or cocktail reception.

*Tutera Tip: Have one music vendor do it all. When hiring many different
entertainment companies, things get confusing. Have the
same vendor provide you with the music for each part of your
wedding: If you want a harpist for your ceremony, a trio for
your cocktail hour, and a band for your reception, keep it in
the family under the same company umbrella. It will be more
organized and you can potentially save money this way.*

Least Expensive—"Finely Tuned" Budgeting

If playing it cost-effectively is sweet music to your ears, then hiring a DJ is your best bet. But don't assume that live music is out completely—some of the greatest performers are the most cost-friendly. Hire a church choir or a local children's choir (or even one great vocalist you can find by word of mouth) to perform to add something extra at your ceremony.

Your Dress

Some brides include their gown in the wedding budget, and some purchase it as a gift from parents or as a personal buy. Whether it is part of the overall budget or not, you know what you should be able to spend on your gown and your job is to stay true to that price (tempting though it may be to fall in love with the couture gorgeousness you saw in the window at a department store or on a magazine cover!).

When shopping, be clear and firm with the sales staff about what your budget is (just like in the real estate market, they may try to show you something above what your budget is to tempt you, but you are too savvy for that!). As far as seeing gowns by price; start low and work your way up. You may fall in love with a gown you see that is below your maximum budget that you'd never notice if you went straight to the couture section.

Here's why it's so important to control your gown spending: When budgeting for a wedding dress, brides always forget the extra costs that come with it. Alterations, veil, shoes, purse, slip, undergarments, and headpiece are all expenses that you don't want to be surprised by—and they can add up. If you will need alterations, ask for an estimate before you buy a dress. Some require more work (and are more costly) than others!

Tutera Tip: Beware when buying online! Some Web sites offer great bargains, but others compromise quality. You need to see, touch, feel, and wear your gown before you even consider purchasing it. I always tell my brides to take the extra time, go into a boutique, see what you like, and then look for matching bargains. Experience the tradition of going to a bridal salon and save the online purchasing for your favors—not your dress. And don't believe everything you see being advertised as a deal—when it comes to your gown, this deserves the extra effort from the dressmakers and from you to find the best service.

- Ask bridal departments and salons if there are any special sales coming up (or if department-store credit cards or incentives will work on gowns!).
- If you find a gown with slight imperfections (loose threads, a broken zipper, lace that needs to be patched), instead of ruling it out, ask the salon if they will fix it for free or give you a percentage off.
- See if smaller boutiques may be able to give you a bargain—if you buy all your accessories in one place they may come down in price.
- Ask if they have a no-interest, layaway payment plan and free storage services until your wedding day.
- See if there are any upcoming designer trunk shows that may be offering special prices.
- See what's included—steaming and pressing? Delivery?

Your Cake

Cakes can be quite costly, so ask potential bakers (or "cake designers," as they are often called) if they can suggest any ways to bring down the price. A multitiered fondant cake with royal icing and sugar-sculpted roses is sure to be much pricier than a smaller-scale buttercream cake piped with pretty decorations—and it might be just as beautiful to you and your guests! Your florist may provide complimentary flowers to add to your cake that will tie it in to the overall look of your ceremony, preventing you from having to pay for the cake designer to create details and intricacies you can do without.

Meet with several bakers. Go in for tastings to try out their goods (and to enjoy a quick treat!). Give yourself financial options; get quotes for different sizes, styles, and ingredients. Local bakers may not make cakes as grandiose as those made by wedding cake specialists, but they may taste even better—which is what matters to your guests in the end! Also remember that simple wedding cakes can be just as beautiful as elaborately decorated ones—and they will certainly be more affordable.

Tutera Tip: *Fake the cake! Online and in specialty stores, there are gorgeous "fake cakes" for rent. Realistically decorated and beautifully adorned to match your wedding, these faux wedding cakes are made for display only (with a small section to cut into for show!). Hidden in the back, servers will pre-cut sheet cakes and serve for a dessert illusion that will save you hundreds and will be just as yummy for your guests.*

Tutera Tip: *If you are serving desserts other than just your wedding cake, do not order a cake size that is based on guest count. Not all guests will eat cake if there are other alternatives, so order to feed 30 percent fewer people than your guest count. If the cake is the only dessert that will be served, do order to the count.*

SMARTLY SPEND, SMARTLY SAVE

- If you are having a groom's cake, ask for a package deal for the baker to do both. There's no need to order a slice of both for each person; combine the amount of cake both cakes provide and order one piece per person.
- See if your venue or caterer will provide a cake at a discounted rate or as part of the overall per-person price.
- Ask what's included in your cake price. Does it include delivery and setup?

Hair and Makeup

How much can you afford to spend on hair and makeup? You need to provide not only for yourself, but for your bridesmaids, flower girl, and mother and mother-in-law. Make sure you first properly consider how many people you need to pay for before you hire a stylist based on how much they will cost to do just you.

SMARTLY SPEND, SMARTLY SAVE

- What is the cost for a trial? Remember, you will pay for each trial, so the more trials you have, the more money you will spend.
- Is the fee per hour or per person being worked upon?
- How many hair and makeup artists do you realistically need to do up your bridal party?
- Does the price include someone on call that night to do touch-ups (especially before pictures if you are taking them in between your ceremony and reception)?

Transportation

Riding in style is a fun luxury for the bride and groom. While it may be well deserved, if cuts need to be made, transportation can be an area where you can scale down. Your first priority is guest convenience, and your second is arriving in high fashion.

In planning your budget for transportation, your location, guest count, and bridal party size play a key role. If your location is difficult to find or far away, a charter bus to grant your guests easy arrival and departure (especially after alcohol consumption) is a must. The larger your bridal party, the more expensive your transportation accommodations will be. If your venue is nearby and your guests don't need to go on an expedition to find it, you're fine with scratching this expense and leaving it up to them to get themselves there.

If providing transportation for your bridal party is necessary, compare prices for limos, minivans, and "party buses." Look for vintage or sports cars to rent. Alternative forms of transportation for a fun, nontraditional spin can be cost-effective and unique—renting rickshaws, trolleys, or mopeds provide great photo opportunities and leave you with style on a dime.

Lighting and Sound

Hiring a lighting company puts the icing on the cake when it comes to the look of your party. Lighting, while often seen as an extra, is actually one of the most dynamic and impressive elements you can add to your reception room; the key is in knowing to ask for the right things to get the desired effect without spending a fortune.

If your venue is a ballroom, hotel, or church space, the venue may do the lighting themselves, either complimentary or for a minimal cost. Lighting can be elaborate and beautiful, but to stay cost-conservative, all you need is some strategically placed shine on focal points of your event:

- Your entertainment
- Dance floor
- Guest tables
- Your cake and/or sweetheart table
- Your important dances (with a spotlight)
- The walls (with a color wash)
- The focal point of where you'll be standing at your ceremony (if the company can do a little more)

If you're bringing in your own lighting company, have a consultation and ask them to show you what they mean by each lighting element they are charging you for. Discuss with them what is most important and what can be negotiated. Indoor and outdoor weddings have different lighting needs for both aesthetics and guest accommodation (no eating and dancing in the dark!).

If you can't afford lighting (though I think it makes *all* the difference), use tons of candlelight, and ask your venue if they have dimmer switches to avoid using the houselights all night (too bright!). You can't go wrong with an abundance of candles. Large groupings of them around your ceremony and on your cocktail and reception tables is the way to go (but do check the rules and regulations of candle use with your venue).

SMARTLY SPEND, SMARTLY SAVE

- Are there any setup or breakdown fees?
- Will someone be on-site in case he or she needs to rewire something? How much will having that person cost?
- Do you need to work with a certain company that your venue recommends? If so, find out that cost before signing your venue contract.
- What is included in your contract?
- What will everything actually look like? You decide the color, light texture, and overall appearance . . . but don't assume that a light pink wash is actually the light pink you imagine. (You may envision a blush pink but they may install fuchsia! There are hundreds of shades of pink, as well as other colors.) Test out your lighting and ask them their professional opinion based on your clear description of what you want and the overall space.

Accessories

Accessorizing your wedding is just like accessorizing yourself when getting all dolled up: You wait to do this last, after first getting all the absolutely necessary pieces together. The end is when you add the frills, sparkles, and finishing touches. Once you get to this point, you know you are almost done!

This category is where I fear brides go wild, mainly because brides do *not* wait until the end to do the finishing touches, and they buy throughout the planning process. All the small things do add up, from monogrammed votives to mints-in-a-tin, to key-chain favors, kissing bells, bubbles to blow, butterflies to launch, gift-card boxes covered in lace and trim, personalized candies, aisle bows, "It's my wedding and you're going to like it" T-shirts, wedding-cake toppers, cake cutters and servers, toasting flutes, guest books, bridal memory books, spa trips for your bridal attendants and money-clip thank-you gifts for your groomsmen, special ring bearer pillows and flower girl baskets, unity candles, garters, jewelry and tiaras and hairpieces, oh my! From personalized BeDazzled undergarments to live doves to sit around in white cages and coo at your guests, I've seen it *all*. Accessories are a serious money trap, and it's very important for you to avoid draining all your savings. It's easy to think that accessories are all small purchases that don't fall under any budget category, but they are big enough when combined that they get one of their own! (And some of those accessories can get pret-ty expensive at bridal boutiques just waiting to tempt brides!)

The best advice I have is to be patient. So many brides waste money by buying things twice because they've discovered that a "cute" impulse purchase doesn't fit in at the end! Be strong! Resist making your wedding too themed. And always think of the overall wedding picture (lookwise and budgetwise).

Venue Rental

When you're selecting a venue, you're also determining your budget in other aspects and you may not know it! When you go to a space that has nothing, your budget will have to be larger because you have to bring everything in: tables, chairs, chinaware, glassware and flatware, dance floor, lighting, sound, and sometimes kitchen equipment—everything from scratch. Look for a venue that has these items in stock, and you will save yourself a bundle in both money and effort by not needing to source these items on your own.

Venues range greatly in price. If you marry in your parish or synagogue, prices may be none to minimal, while if you head to a hotel ballroom, you are talking more money. Weigh the pros and cons of each venue and calculate how much it would cost to have the venue and supply the rest of the items (party rentals, decor, etc.). It is not possible to compare venue fee to venue fee. You have to compare venue fees *and* what the venue provides, and what you will have to provide yourself, for each one. While venue is not necessarily the most expensive part of your budget, it needs to be the first step you take in preparing your wedding budget, as it leads to other decisions you will or won't have to make.

Tutera Tip: What may appear expensive as far as venue charges when you see it as "price per person" may actually not be when you see what you get!

SMARTLY SPEND, SMARTLY SAVE

- What vendors can you work with? When you go into a venue, always ask them this. If the location contractually has to work with exclusive vendors, sometimes you won't be able to negotiate better deals for your party. That "great" price they are charging you may turn out to be more than you thought on the back end. Know all the information about the venue before signing on the dotted line.

- What is the overtime charge for the venue? Is it counted as every thirty minutes or an hour?

- What is included? Having the venue during setup and breakdown times? Cleaning fees? Valet? Coat check? Bathroom attendants? These are typically priced out separately than the per-person fee, so question their costliness.

- Can you make a donation to the venue's preservation society or nonprofit organization (which is then tax-deductible) in lieu of paying a rental fee? This is most applicable to museums and other public venues.

Tipping

When you throw an event, it's customary to tip certain vendors for their services. Who do you tip and how much?

That Little Something Extra

Once you have developed your entire budget, add 10 percent of it to your final total as a cushion, for "extras and unpredictables." You

Vendor/Position	Expected Gratuity (percentage of their fees)	Note
Caterer/Banquet Manager	15–20%	This is usually included in the contract, but if you feel as though he/she has done an exceptional job, an additional $2–4 dollars per guest is suggested.
Waitstaff	15–20%	Prior to your event, check with the venue if the gratuity included in your contract is actually a gratuity or simply the money put toward the staff's paychecks.
Limousine/Transportation Drivers	15–20%	
DJ	15%	Gratuities are not usually required; however, if he/she does an exceptional job, 15% of the total contract is suggested.
Bands	$50 per band member	
Hair & Makeup Artist	15–20%	
Lady-in-Waiting	10%	
Parking Attendants/ Valet	$1–2 per car	
Wedding Planner/ Design Coordinator	15–20%	

never know what may surface that is unavoidable, and you don't want to go overbudget if something turns up unexpectedly. If you end up not using it—put it toward your new home!

BUDGETING WITH VENDORS

Try to negotiate with vendors, but also keep in mind you are getting a service—not just tangible goods. You want to get the best price for yourself, while also respecting your vendor's services. Think of it as somewhere between haggling for a fake Prada on a corner of Fifth

Avenue and discussing a peace treaty at the United Nations. You want to develop a wedding team that will look out for you and want to make you happy! (Remember, you attract more bees with honey than with vinegar!)

Trust your vendors and don't micromanage; it will stifle their creativity. But do check in with friendly reminders, questions, and meetings. Make it more social than "hounding" them. That being said, vendors have a responsibility to you, too, and should not add stress to your life—they should be making it easier and making you comfortable as a client (you are paying *them*). They are in the business of making you look great, and you are in the business of throwing a great wedding, so these relationships should strike a harmonious chord. Ask questions. Do walk-throughs with them and set up meetings to ensure you are on the same page, financially and conceptually. Do not feel rushed to sign a contract with a vendor, but also keep in mind you need to give them time to properly execute your services (they are vendors, not genies). Respect and information sharing from both sides is the trick.

Tutera Tip: Be careful of vendors that may add in hidden expenses in the end. Additional labor or overtime costs, breakdown charges, fees for lost or damaged items . . . These are all things to watch out for postwedding.

THE STRESS-FREE BRIDE-TO-BE

The purpose of all this planning is to help you think of everything by the time your wedding comes, so that you have no surprises and are able to afford a beautiful wedding that fits your style and doesn't break the bank. Because you are taking these precautionary steps, don't get overwhelmed—you are saving yourself from getting a headache later when you will have much more important things to focus on—like having a great time with your new husband, family, and friends!

And if all else fails and you find yourself in a bind over what you should spend your extra money on and what you shouldn't—remember, your budget is to be tailored to what *you* like and what you value—pull out that priority list we made earlier and remember how you felt when you were thinking from the heart.

BUDGET PLANNER

PRINTED MATERIALS

_____ SAVE-THE-DATE CARDS

_____ INVITATION AND ENVELOPES

_____ PROGRAMS

_____ ESCORT CARDS, PLACE CARDS, TABLE NUMBERS, AND MENU CARDS

_____ INVITES FOR SHOWERS, ENGAGEMENT PARTIES, REHEARSAL DINNER, BRUNCHES

_____ THANK-YOU NOTES

_____ POSTAGE

_____ CALLIGRAPHY

_____ ANNOUNCEMENTS

_____ FAVOR BOXES/TAGS

_____ COCKTAIL NAPKINS AND BATHROOM TOWELS

Subtotal: $ _____

FASHION

_____ BRIDE'S DRESS

_____ HEADPIECE AND VEIL

_____ BRIDE'S SHOES

_____ LINGERIE/UNDERGARMENTS

(continued)

_____ JEWELRY AND ACCESSORIES

_____ HAIR AND MAKEUP

_____ MANICURE AND PEDICURE

_____ GROOM'S TUXEDO OR SUIT

_____ GROOM'S ACCESSORIES

_____ BRIDE'S AND GROOM'S RINGS

_____ ALTERATIONS AND DRY-CLEANING

_____ BRIDESMAIDS' FASHION AND ACCESSORIES

_____ GROOMSMEN'S FASHION AND ACCESSORIES

Subtotal: $ _____

MUSIC

_____ PRE-CEREMONY MUSIC

_____ CEREMONY MUSIC

_____ COCKTAIL-HOUR MUSIC

_____ RECEPTION MUSIC

_____ AFTER-PARTY MUSIC

Subtotal: $ _____

PHOTOGRAPHY/VIDEOGRAPHY

_____ PHOTOGRAPHER'S FEE

_____ ENGAGEMENT PORTRAITS

_____ WEDDING ALBUM

_____ PARENTS' ALBUMS

_____ ADDITIONAL PRINTS

_____ VIDEOGRAPHER'S FEE

_____ VIDEO/DVD COPIES

Subtotal: $ _____

FLOWERS/DECOR

_____ CEREMONY DECORATIONS

_____ BRIDE'S BOUQUET

_____ MAID/MATRON OF HONOR'S AND BRIDESMAIDS' BOUQUETS

_____ FLOWER GIRL'S ACCESSORIES

_____ CORSAGES

_____ BOUTONNIERES

_____ RECEPTION CENTERPIECES AND DECORATIONS

_____ TABLE LINENS

_____ LIGHTING

Subtotal: $ _____

CEREMONY, RECEPTION, AND LOGISTICS

_____ WEDDING PLANNER FEE, IF USING

_____ CEREMONY LOCATION FEE

_____ OFFICIANT'S FEE

_____ MARRIAGE LICENSE

_____ RECEPTION-SITE FEE

_____ FOOD

_____ CAKE

_____ BAR

_____ RENTALS

_____ COUPLE'S TRANSPORTATION

_____ BRIDAL PARTY TRANSPORTATION

_____ GUESTS' TRANSPORTATION AND PARKING

_____ TIPS AND COAT CHECK

Subtotal: $ _____

GIFTS, FAVORS, AND ACCESSORIES

_____ MAID/MATRON OF HONOR'S GIFT

_____ BRIDESMAIDS' GIFTS

_____ BEST MAN'S GIFT

_____ GROOMSMEN'S GIFTS

_____ CHILD ATTENDANTS' GIFTS

(continued)

_____ COUPLE'S GIFTS FOR EACH OTHER

_____ PARENTS' GIFTS

_____ GUEST-ROOM GIFTS

_____ FAVORS

_____ RING PILLOW

_____ GUEST BOOK

_____ AMENITY BASKETS FOR BATHROOMS

Subtotal: $ _____

OVERALL TOTAL: $ _____

Three

SCENE-SETTING FOR YOUR WEDDING

Selecting where and when to hold your wedding is the most important decision a bride can make—after deciding to marry her groom, of course! As you explore your options, take your time and think thoroughly. In this aspect, you have total control over your wedding—including setting the scene and creating the ambience as you wed and then dine, dance, and celebrate your love! Your wedding date, followed by the venue you choose, will paint the picture of your wedding story, from the "scene" where you exchange your vows to the setting in which you dance your first dance as husband and wife. The "where" is not just special but necessary to start telling your wedding story.

THE PERFECT DATE:
CHOOSING WHEN YOUR WEDDING
WILL TAKE PLACE

How do you choose what date is right for your wedding? One of the first decisions you have to make to successfully plan any event is to decide the day. Everything you plan will depend on that date. When you imagine your wedding, what scenario are you in? Perhaps you are outdoors in beautiful weather, or inside your own winter wonderland. Some brides dream of a nighttime summer's eve bash or an autumnal harvest-inspired soiree. The choices are endless, and while I wish I could offer a formula to what time or place will make your wedding dream come true, truth be told, it's simply a matter of you knowing what will work for you and what setting will truly make it feel like *your* wedding. Take the necessary time to figure out when and where . . . and then your story will begin to be told.

Venue. If getting a particular venue is what's most important to you, you may choose a date based upon its availability. For a wedding at a particular venue like a hotel, restaurant, or vineyard, I have found that some days can be less expensive than others. If you take the time to do a comparative analysis, you may find you can save money by choosing Friday night instead of Saturday, or a daytime instead of an evening event. If you're flexible and cost is a concern, look into your options.

Vision. If you are leaving your date up to your vision of the dream day, when you imagine yourself getting married, are you indoors or outdoors? What time of day do you picture it?

Date. Is there a certain date that has meaning to you?

Location. What state/location will you get married in, and when is the best weather there? (A January outdoor wedding in Florida is much different than one in North Dakota!) If you are getting married on a mountain in Aspen, you may want to do so during the fall versus fighting an abominable snowstorm!

Season. Is there a season that you love or a time of year that sparks a certain positive memory? Colors you envision for your wedding can also be indicative of when to wed. Perhaps you are surrounded by bright, cheerful summer colors, or rustic autumn jewel tones. From pretty spring pastels to wintery whites, your color palette can even help you set the date.

Summer Weddings

If sun-drenched days and starlit nights sound just right for your wedding, then you join the many brides and grooms who take advantage of the weather and mood a wedding in the summer season offers.

I DO's for Summer Weddings

- Keep your guests hydrated and cool with bottles of water and fans aplenty at any celebration outdoors, and keep the air-conditioning on full blast indoors. It's easier to keep the heat under control when you start with a cool room before guests arrive.
- You shouldn't be bitten by anything but the love bug; take insect repellant precautions! Put out citronella candles and ask landscaping companies about "bug bombs" you can detonate days before an outdoor wedding to keep pesky unwanted guests at bay. Offer little packets of repellant in a pretty basket to your guests.
- The summer heat brings sweat, so do remember to keep a small beauty bag nearby to touch up makeup or to freshen up with deodorant and perfume.
- Microphone your ceremony if it is near water. The sound of

the water will be heard over your voices, so make sure your loved ones hear your vows!

- Do dessert by a pool, beach, or waterside locale to create a cool change of venue.
- Provide flip-flops or alternative footwear options for your guests for a fun summer wedding (especially a beach wedding in the sand).
- Do a sunset service. Mother Nature paints a glorious picture of color behind you! Research the anticipated sunset time for your wedding date, locate the best spot, and don't run late! You want your guests to be able to see you and your wedding party and enjoy the glow of the sky.

Tutera Tip: Right before sunset there is always a light breeze, especially on the water, so anchor down decor or ceremony programs and other loose items so nothing falls or flies away!

- Check the tides for beach weddings. Full moons reflect the swell of the tides, causing waves and unpredictable issues on your coastline.
- Avoid hurricane season in the areas of the country that are afflicted by destructive weather and difficult travel.

I DON'Ts for Summer Weddings

- Don't take your wedding pictures in the early afternoon. In most parts of the country (especially the South) this is by far the hottest and most humid part of the day. No bride wants to walk into her ceremony or reception after spending hours in the hot sun!
- Avoid an extravagant hairstyle for an outdoor summer wedding, since it might not hold up in the heat and humidity. A simple nice updo is a safer bet.
- In summer, clear tents act like solariums, collecting light and heat from the sun, so steer clear of these in hot months.

- Don't stage a wedding ceremony by a pond or a lake. The bugs attack!
- Afternoon celebrations risk unpredictable summer showers, so don't plan a midday soiree. Summer mornings and nights have a better chance of being dry.
- Don't cut the lawn (and ask your venue not to) the day of; fresh-cut grass will activate allergies of your guests. Achoo!
- Try not to have a park or beach ceremony during the day. Most, if not all, beaches and parks are public spaces, and no bride wants to have Frisbee players, sunbathers, and loud music around the guests and ceremony area.

Fall Weddings

Perhaps a crisp fall day in the cool breeze is the ideal scenario for you. In fall, a beautiful array of changing foliage and richly colored flowers are yours for the taking.

I DO's for Fall Weddings

- The months of September to November can be a bit unpredictable when it comes to weather, so be prepared for both hot and cold weather. As you approach the cooler times of the year, heat lamps in outdoor spaces (once the sun sets) are a must for keeping your guests warm from the chilly nights. Have heaters professionally installed and on hand.
- Have wraps, blankets, and umbrellas available for invited guests—these make great party favors that are usable long after, as well!
- Make sure that outdoor grounds are properly lit so that when the sun goes down, guests can see where they are walking. Also have a groundskeeper sweep a path clear of all debris and/or rocks where guests will be entering and exiting your tent or venue.

- Do incorporate fall elements into decor. Fall brings rich jewel tones and an abundance of textures that can enhance your wedding decor.
- Select a location where nature lends beauty with colors that are revealed at a certain peak time. Find out that time and plan accordingly!
- Do a tent wedding! Fall is the most amazing time of the year for outdoor weather and for natural beauty. A clear tent can enable you to sit underneath canopies of leaves while still dining in a controlled environment.
- An open fire for a dessert party is an idyllic end to a wedding reception. Bring out hot cider and have materials for making s'mores for your guests. Serve cocktails that are autumnal in flavor and presentation (like a "Harvest Spice" cocktail).
- Use readily available seasonal elements. Turn pumpkins into candlesticks: Carve out the tops to display tea light candles or tapers. Leaves can be used for a consistent decor element to tie in with the outside. Carve the bride and groom's monogram into a pumpkin and set it at the escort table, or carve beautiful designs for aisle treatments. Paint pumpkins and gourds metallic gold and copper colors for a lush, sophisticated way to display the season of autumn.
- Offer horse-and-carriage rides through the trees to your destination—perfect for the dream fall wedding.

I DON'Ts for Fall Weddings

- Prevent yourself from accidentally choosing a date on or near a religious or national holiday. During this season, there are a number of them, so check your calendar! Don't make your guests choose between your special day and a family gathering.
- When scheduling your wedding, keep away from dates at the end of the peak of the season. Weather can be unpre-

dictable, and one windy rainstorm can strip you of all the color you dreamed of!

- With decor and color schemes, circumvent the expected orange color palette. Add punches of unique color, like orange with purple and copper. Mix in metallic colors, which are great for autumn, rich in tone, and showy in presentation.
- Don't forget about daylight savings time, and be aware of the sunset during the time change. You don't want to be surprised with a dark night!
- Avoid "overscenting" your venue with richly scented candles or potpourri. It can overwhelm your senses and ruin your taste buds for dinner.
- In fall, don't depend on candlelight only. You want your guests to see the colors of the trees and the great outdoors, so don't forget to highlight areas that are visually amazing with supplemental lighting.

Winter Weddings

Winter weddings are elegant and exciting; this season is a perfect time of year for a wedding as magical as the holidays and the ethereal drift of snow. Crisp, clean, and diamond white "naturally" say bridal, and it's the perfect time of year for family gatherings.

I DO's for Winter Weddings

- Have rich, opulent fashion for your bridesmaids—a luxury for winter weddings! Wraps, shawls, or jackets are wonderful winter accessories.
- Create a visual white wonderland for winter indoors (and you won't have to rely on a snowfall!).
- Add glitter or crystals to flowers, tables, and invites to add a wintry sparkle to white winter wedding elements.
- For weddings taking place in potentially snowy weather, choose a venue such as a hotel where guests can choose to stay overnight in case of anticipated bad road conditions

due to snowy/icy weather. If possible, choose a venue in a metropolis with plenty of public transportation alternatives for your guests.

- Have an inclement-weather plan in case of a snowstorm the day of your wedding. If a blizzard occurs, you may have to delay the start time of your wedding. Give your guests time to arrive safely. Allow realistic space in your timeline for vendors to get through storms and then set up without rushing.

- Be cognizant of the weather warnings to keep your guests safe and off the roads as much as possible. If your venue area is infamous for blizzards (or if one is predicted— research as much as you can), then consider a new date for sunnier skies and stronger guest turnout. If you are in the clear, ask the venue and others in the area your wedding will be held in what happens when there is a great storm, so you know if your roads will be passable in case Mother Nature decides to attend, too! Try to have your ceremony, cocktail hour, and reception in one venue to keep unnecessary travel to a minimum. Make sure your venue is adequately heated, and your guests' time outdoors is limited.

- Ensure that your venue has a coat check and an attendant to accommodate your guests' extra layers.

I DON'Ts for Winter Weddings

- Don't choose an out-of-the-way venue . . . you may have always wanted that winter cabin wedding at a tucked-away little inn, but bad road conditions could prevent your guests from getting to your wedding.

- Don't get your heart set on flowers that may be out of season, impossible to obtain, or available but extremely expensive during this time of year. Ask your florist what wedding-oriented flowers are available in winter.

- Don't go with an all-white menu, which, while in theme with the color of the season, ends up being visually disappointing and unappetizing. Choose colorful foods and garnishes with flavored and colored sorbet and exciting, vibrant dishes.

- Don't encourage your caterer to serve heavy "winter" food for your dinner menu. Thick sauces and heavier meats belong in this season, but for your wedding, keep your menu seasonal without being too overbearing so your guests still feel light enough on their feet to dance.
- Christmas lights belong on Christmas trees (though they have a tendency to pop up on topiaries and ficus trees in hotel ballrooms and venue spaces!). As temptingly twinkly as they may be to you, please just say no when it comes to your wedding and keep the upscale, sophisticated look you're going for in perspective.

Spring Weddings

Spring is a time of new beginnings, when love is in the air for certain . . . not to mention, the decor options are limitless with the all the flowers in bloom and the weather becoming warm for the first time in months! (It's no wonder that spring is the most popular time of the year to get married!)

I DO's for Spring Weddings

- Make your vendor and venue reservations as early as possible to secure them before the wedding rush!
- Create a spectacular spring menu. Try an amazing salad with pansy accents. Do a lavender martini or champagne infused with rose syrup as a specialty drink.
- With your bridesmaid dresses, choose shades of a color palette and accent with a colored wrap or accessories.
- Use butterflies and dragonflies as beautiful accents. From pretty paper ornaments to molded chocolate favors, these elegant signs of spring add a charming touch of the outdoors.
- Keep spring weather in mind when planning your dress or the bridesmaid dresses. Spring weather can be hot one

minute and cold the next. Keep a nice wrap handy for when it gets chilly.

- Choose bouquets that are monochromatic in color, light and airy for spring. Enjoy spring flowers; it's the best time of year for amazing florals: peonies, flowering branches, sweet peas, tulips . . . the selection in spring is endless, so take advantage!

I DON'Ts for Spring Weddings

- It is more likely to rain in the spring, so don't choose the wrong material for your and your bridesmaids' dresses and shoes. Nix satin and suede, and other materials that are not very water-resistant!
- Don't wait until the last minute to decide on a location and a date. May and June are wedding-heavy, so your wedding day may be the same day as other brides getting married. Your guests may be doing double duty and going to two weddings in one day, or they may have to choose which to attend, so give them a bit more notice than normal to help them plan.
- Your venues may be trying to put on more than one wedding at a time, so don't pick a day when there are sure to be many competing events. Prepare to be as organized as possible! If you must choose a venue that holds more than one event at a time, check to see what other events are going on when yours is. Spring is also prom season, so ask what's going on in nearby ballrooms. (You may love kids, but the last thing any bride wants is for the local high school to be holding its annual prom right next door to her reception!)
- If you're having your reception in a location with multiple weddings occurring on the same day, make sure the start times are staggered. Avoid using the same entrance as other brides to prevent guest confusion (some venues have sepa-

rate entrances when housing multiple events). We don't want any strangers at your party!

Tutera Tip: Use the seasons to your advantage, but keep your guests as comfortable as possible, in heat or cold. Your guests need to be as content as you are.

THAT SPECIAL TIME OF YEAR: HOLIDAY WEDDINGS

I have very strong feelings about selecting a wedding date that coincides with a national or religious holiday. Weekends like Memorial Day, which for most people is considered the first official weekend of summer, and Labor Day, traditionally the last weekend of the summer, are challenging dates to host a wedding due to the popularity of travel plans and accommodation difficulties. Give as much notice as possible to your guests through save-the-date cards, because people plan their family vacations and out-of-town trips far in advance. The advantage is that some guests will see this as perfect timing since they won't have to take off personal days from work if they need to travel to your nuptials. Others, however, may be put off because they cannot attend due to a yearly family vacation or reunion (as these are popular weekends for family travel). Your Rsvps will see both results.

There are advantages and disadvantages to having your wedding on other notable holidays: Valentine's Day, the Fourth of July, Christmas Eve, and New Year's Eve are all memorable days that can make your celebration even more special (and ensure you never, ever forget your anniversary). I personally believe your wedding should be a special day of celebration on its own and not shared with anything else! But if you have your heart set on a holiday wedding, here's what you need to look out for:

Unpredictable Guest Count. If you are making wedding plans for a major holiday, you might keep your guest list to just close family and friends, as holidays are usually reserved for family members and your guest count may suffer because of their significance to others. Also, traveling to your wedding would be incongruous with long-held plans or traditions. So if you want a major holiday wedding, I say keep it a small and intimate celebration. It is likely you will receive more declines in Rsvps than you would for a nonholiday wedding: The general rule of thumb is that 10 to 15 percent of your guests decline, but for a holiday wedding, plan for that percentage to be greater.

Increased Expenses. Flowers are insanely expensive on Valentine's Day and around Mother's Day, and floral companies are very busy (and prices go up) during the winter holidays. (Holidays are also big spending times for people, and they may not be able to easily splurge on attending a wedding, as well.)

Overtime Charges. Your vendor costs also may go up if it is a holiday and the vendors need to pay their employees overtime . . . which means *you* may be paying those employees overtime (and that is not a way to bring in holiday joy!).

Travel. Hotels are pricey and airfare is often increased around holidays, so consider this before finalizing your wedding date and your budget. Travel is also more expensive during peak vacation times and may be financially inconvenient for guests coming from afar, which will deter your turnout.

I DO's for a Holiday Wedding

- Own the holiday-inspired theme without going overboard. Why have a holiday wedding if you're going to throw a celebration that ignores the holiday? Make subtle nods to the special day that you are sharing your wedding with. For example, a New Year's Eve wedding could have a variety of gorgeous antique clocks as part of the decor and theme.

- Utilize elements available in the season: winter spices, spring flowers, summer weather, or the fall harvest are all great ways to incorporate the time of year without bringing in Santa and the Easter Bunny.

- Decide if "holiday-color chic" is really the way you want to go. Is a "red, white, and blue" wedding what you really want? (Hint: No!) I suggest extracting one of the holiday theme colors and working with that for your wedding so it's connected to the holiday without being too literal. For example, choose just blues and whites for your July Fourth weekend wedding, and if you must have the red, choose a deep burgundy and use it very sparingly.

- Be sure to check with the venue where you are thinking of having your holiday wedding to make sure they are not having an event of their own. Some venues open their doors to the public on holidays such as New Year's Eve and host their own events.

- Make sure to speak to the vendors you are considering to see if they are available on these holidays. Some vendors do close for certain vacations or times of the year.

I DON'Ts for a Holiday Wedding

- Please don't play music that is seasonal to the holiday. A touch of Christmas carols through cocktails works, but when it comes to the rest of your entertainment, it's time to stop. You want your guests to feel like they are at a wedding, not a big holiday party. (If you have "Grandma Got Run Over by a Reindeer" playing at any time during your wedding, I'm sending a man in a big red suit to your wedding, to deliver you coal.)

IN A FARAWAY LAND:
DESTINATION WEDDINGS

From the beaches of the Caribbean to the vineyards of Napa, from a bed-and-breakfast in Boston or a chic city celebration in Chicago . . . destination weddings are growing in popularity now more than ever. The amount of fun that goes along with a traveling wedding is paralleled by the variables and planning, so as you choose your dream destination, keep these tips in mind!

I DO's for Destination Weddings

- Be aware of "peak" and "off-peak" seasons. Peak season will be more expensive because you will be competing with crowded resorts and lots of visitors, so an off-peak season may be better for seclusion . . . but don't be fooled; there is a reason off-peak has its name. During off-peak season, some destination resorts may have great prices, but it's because they are undergoing renovation and not all the amenities are open (restaurants are closed, tourist shops and spas may be closed, it might not be full-service etc.). Ask your resort specifically before booking so you are not bringing yourself and your guests to an environment of bad surprises.
- Check to see if your wedding date needs to revolve around your dream resort's wedding-space and room availability for your guests' accommodations. Speak to the hotel that will be hosting your wedding about setting up a room block well in advance so that your guests get a discounted room rate.
- Offer multiple hotel and accommodation choices that vary in price. Choose a host hotel (a main hotel, likely where you are holding your ceremony and where you are staying yourselves), and two other choices. Your guests will greatly appreciate this!

- Consider when the majority of your guests will be able to travel. You want the best turnout possible.

- Choose a neutral location that doesn't favor either side of the family (if you dream of getting married in your native homeland of Puerto Rico and his entire family resides in Texas, the expenses for guest travel would be quite skewed!). Some locations are also more difficult to get to than others, regardless of personal ties, so when choosing the ideal location, make sure your guests can easily get to it (for example, Napa, California, is more difficult to reach through flights and drives than flying directly into Miami and being in the heart of it all).

- When considering destinations be sure to look up the weather for that part of the region in the season you are planning to have your wedding. For tropical destinations, your wedding might be during hurricane season or the hottest time of the year; you don't want you and your guests to be caught up in a storm (or stuck at the resort, in an airport, or in danger). If you always wanted to get married in the Rocky Mountains, you need to make sure you don't need a snowplow for you and your guests to get there!

- If the ceremony is taking place outside near water, do check for high and low tides and the phases of the moon. You don't want your ceremony to get washed out!

- Send out save-the-date cards to all your anticipated guests. This gives your friends and relatives plenty of time to make travel arrangements. Take into account that some guests might have to bring small children. Make sure to ask your hosting hotel about babysitting services and their rates.

- Keep your veil short to make it manageable in the ocean winds or breezy locales.

- Always be thinking about how comfortable your guests will be. Do select a destination where temperature is comfortable—not extreme! Provide guests with information on your destination, including altitude, temperature, and suggested clothing.

* Consult with a travel agent and select a destination with many choices of airlines and flight times. If you make it easy for your guests to say yes, they will be there!

I DON'Ts for Destination Weddings

* Try not to choose locations that are only accessible by boat. Some of your guests might opt not to attend since they might not be comfortable on the high seas!

* Avoid finding yourself far from home without wedding help: Don't assume that the event person on-site at your venue will be available to you at all times. It is always best to hire a wedding planner to make sure that the day of your wedding runs smoothly and without mishaps.

* Don't mix sand and heels! If your wedding is taking place on a soft sandy beach, trade your stilettos for elegant flip-flops, go barefoot, or keep the high heels and install a platform for your ceremony stage and your aisle for the comfort and ease of the people in the processional.

* Don't expect that a large variety of flowers will be available to you at your specific location. Speak to your planner and/or floral designer about the options you will have for your planned destination. Know their expertise before assuming they can execute your designs.

* Don't put important valuables like the wedding rings in your luggage and check it at the airport. Keep these things on you at all times.

* Don't go too far away! How remote is your destination and what do you need for your wedding? The more remote, the more expensive it will be to import your vendors, foods, florals, and other elements you need to provide. Shipping long distances also takes up time and requires extra planning for on-time arrivals.

- Don't have your honeymoon at the same destination location as your wedding. Say good-bye and depart to somewhere that is just for you. Guests may want to linger (and they will be encroaching on your honeymoon if they are chilling out with you by the pool all week!).

- Don't make your destination require two forms of transportation for your guests; things may come out being confusing and costly for them and for you. (But that sounds like a great remote honeymoon destination instead to me!)

- Don't be at the wrong place at the wrong time! Are there any festivals or national celebrations coming up you should be aware of that may make travel difficult, or may detract from your event?

- Don't overplan or underplan your guests' time. Give them downtime to explore the destination themselves. Is there nightlife for them and activities if they choose to turn your wedding into a vacation?

- No sleeping during your destination wedding! Dodge the drowsiness of jet lag and provide one day of arrival time for you and your guests to get acclimated to the location.

Destination: Wedding

When having a destination wedding, make sure you host the three main components. On day one, it's customary for the bride and groom (or their parents) to hold an arrival party for your guests (this could also double as your rehearsal dinner). Choose a unique off-site venue, and welcome your fellow travelers among food and cocktails. For the actual wedding day, keep it simple! Have the ceremony and reception on-site and enjoy the destination for what it is. Last, right before you and your guests depart, have an on-site (easily accessible to outgoing travelers) send-off brunch to bid your guests farewell with fond memories of their trip with you.

LOCATION, LOCATION, LOCATION: SELECTING A CEREMONY AND RECEPTION VENUE

As they say: It's all about location, location, location! We have the when and the why—now let's figure out the *where*! You may have already had the dream venue chosen for eons, but if you haven't, your first task is to choose an indoor wedding versus an outdoor wedding.

The Great Outdoors: Weddings in a Natural Setting

The beauty of nature and the great outdoors speaks enough for itself. In fact, many couples—about 35 percent—get married outside. Whether you are under a great blue sky (or a blanket of stars) or a tent built just for your occasion, being outside allows you to have many scenic opportunities with little effort. The rolling hills of a vineyard? An ocean breeze? A romantic, enchanted forest by candlelight? Your decor is already there.

PROS TO OUTDOOR WEDDINGS
- Natural beautiful settings
- The ability to choose an area or venue that has special meaning to you (like the backyard of a home where you grew up)
- The overall views and no need for lots of outsourced decor
- Gardens in spring and summer, natural blooming flowers, mountains with autumn colors, and other picturesque surroundings
- Opportunities for more space

While there are many pros to being in the great outdoors, the cons need to be recognized as you plan so you can avoid them (or plan for them) as much as possible!

CONS TO OUTDOOR WEDDINGS

- Extra fees to have certain things on hand such as tents, heaters, and/or air conditioners
- The need for ample "unnaturals"—power supplies, lighting, and generators; this could be quite costly due to rentals, sometimes even twice as much as doing it inside!
- Extra expense for catering if an outdoor kitchen needs to be erected specifically for your wedding
- Having to build your event from scratch—everything from guest tables and chairs to the dance floor and restrooms will need to be rented
- Having to apply for permits within a certain amount of time, which is also an added expense
- Bugs
- Difficult accessibility to venue for vendors and guests
- Lack of toilets and level ground

Tutera Tip: If doing an outdoor tented or garden wedding, try to select level, higher ground.

- Unpredictable weather (so you'll need a rain plan and it's possible you will use it!)
- Potential for a sound ordinance, which will mean having to end your event earlier than you wish

Rain, Rain, Go Away: Rain Plans

No matter what outdoor location you are considering, be prepared with a rain plan. If there is a 30 percent chance of rain, your plan should go into effect. Track the weather on Web sites. Know your area's past weather history and tendencies for the time of year so you understand what kind of environment you are working with. Do not be stranded in the middle of nowhere without protective coverings from rain, wind, and snow. Safety and comfort is crucial for both you in your pretty white dress and your guests!

Rain plans require time to put into action. If you are expecting not-so-great weather for your wedding (and especially if you are having the reception outside under a tent), you should have some items in place in case you need to act quickly and make the rain fun without being a downer:

- Wet vacuum
- Large golf umbrellas
- High-rubber rain boots for guests
- Plastic tarps and plastic bags to transport items indoors

Make the situation work for you as best you can: Buy cute rain accessories to help your guests enjoy the inclement weather as much as possible. Have a basket at the entrance of your tent and invite ladies to remove high-heeled shoes in exchange for boots! Purchase umbrellas in your wedding colors. Clear ponchos are affordable and can be "served" on a silver tray or in a basket. Towels on hand for guests to dry off with can be in your colors, folded in creative ways, or, if paper, printed with your monogram.

If the weather is really bad for the ceremony and reception and you must move the wedding to an indoor location, create a buffet dinner with pieces of existing furniture. Still have the caterers serve people and make sure to pass plenty of drinks.

Outdoor Tented Weddings

A tented party offers a blank canvas. You can create a more customized look and feel with a tented space because you start from the ground up—literally! But be warned that tents in general can result in the highest level of stress a host can endure. We've all heard of nightmare stories of tents that leak, blow away, and even collapse on the crowd (for fun-filled tent disasters, rent the movies *Betsy's Wedding* and *Father of the Bride!*). Hiring tenting professionals will help guarantee a successful wedding, so make sure that if you choose to have a tented event, you are working with a competent vendor. Have them do a complete site inspection of your property to make sure that the chosen land is appropriate for the construction and that you have a reliable power source to satisfy the electrical needs of your party. Also make sure you have space for guest parking and for the building of a kitchen if your caterer needs to serve from outside.

Tutera Tip: Tenting can get expensive, due to the cost of the following elements you must provide on top of your other wedding expenses to have a successful tented affair: lighting; flooring, carpet, and dance floor; rentals of tables, chairs, and china; staging; air conditioning and/or heating; power generators.

Tutera Tip: Most communities require permits for tents to be constructed. You also may be legally bound to provide emergency-exit signage and fire extinguishers. You also should research regulations regarding open flames and flameproof materials if you are considering candlelight in a tent.

YOUR DEFINING MOMENT: A TENT GLOSSARY

Pole Tents are constructed with a series of center poles and quarter poles (shorter poles that bring the ceiling lower toward the perimeter) supporting the overhead tent. While this is the most cost-effective of tents, there are also pole structures in the middle of the tented area that cannot be moved, which may be undesirable to party throwers. The number of poles used is determined by how large your tent is: The bigger the tent, the more the poles.

Century Tents. Sleek and sturdy, the century tent is constructed with tenting material stretched tightly over poles for a more elegant look. Center poles must be used to support the aerodynamic design, but the inside of the tent is more like being inside a building than outside in a tent.

Tutera Tip: One of my favorite ways to do a tent is with a clear ceiling, made out of a clear vinyl that makes the sky and your surroundings part of your decor! Clear tents make a tent not feel as closed in, and are perfect for outdoor weddings that take place among beautiful foliage, sunsets, or natural backdrops. There is an up charge for the clear material, but it may be worth it for your wedding.

Structure Tents. Created like the structure of a building, almost as if you were building the framework of a large room, this tent has fabric stretched to fit around its "roof." While they are more labor-intensive to erect, the dilemma of having a center pole in the middle of your wedding reception is solved. The most impressive and most expensive of tenting structures, the structure tent yields a band-shell shape with an open-space interior.

YOUR DEFINING MOMENT: A FLOORING STYLE GLOSSARY

Grass. Using the ground as natural flooring is always an easy option, as long as you take safety into account and make sure the ground and flooring are both level and dry.

Roll-out. A strong plastic mat covering with patterned open grooves is ideal for weather proofing but also a concern for high-heeled shoes.

Subfloor. The construction of an actual floor (wood with supports) evens out the ground and creates a hard surface.

Carpet. Actual carpeting, Astroturf, and other flooring materials are installed for roomlike flooring.

Marquis Tenting. A tented walkway addition. A marquis can also lead to an area of restrooms enclosed by a separate tent, which is always a good idea to discreetly hide restrooms from open view of guests.

Tutera Tip: Ask for a beautiful draped and lined ceiling. Your designer or some tent companies can do this for you. Also ask your tent company about providing staging as part of their setup.

SIZE MATTERS: CHOOSING THE DIMENSIONS OF YOUR TENT

When choosing the size of your tent, the standard guidelines are:

* Dinner reception with dancing: 15 to 17 square feet per person
* Reception with no dancing: 10 square feet per person
* Stand-up cocktail party: 6 square feet per person
* Seating for a ceremony: 7 square feet per person, plus space for aisles and alters

Tutera Tip: Ask for ten-foot-high sides versus eight-foot-high sides. This will literally raise the roof and open up your space.

Safe and Sound: Indoor Weddings

Indoor weddings and receptions are significantly more popular, mainly because they take the guesswork out of the most unpredictable element of your wedding that no amount of planning can fully control: the weather. While it's said that rain on your wedding day is good luck, I think staying dry and keeping things smoothly sailing is also a fortunate circumstance! Indoors, you have the ability to rely on a safe, controlled environment, but you also have to bring a lot into the space to make it your own.

PROS OF INDOOR WEDDINGS

* No bugs
* No rain

- Controlled temperature: no heat or cold to contend with
- The ability to truly create your scenario within the room you rent
- Smaller budget
- No need to consider sunset times or outdoor lighting
- No added expense for exterior lighting or generators
- More availability of the things you need, including tables, staging, dance floor, restrooms, etc.
- An on-site coordinator, who is often included to help you with your plans and/or your execution

CONS OF INDOOR WEDDINGS

- You have the task of transforming a venue into your own personal space
- Your venue may do two weddings a day, so your setup time may be limited
- Multiple weddings taking place at the same time at your venue may add confusion and lessen exclusivity to you
- Sometimes you may not like existing elements that come with the space: chairs, china, room decor, carpeting, wall decor; money is required to change these items—venues do not do this free of charge
- You may love the venue but not the food that comes with it
- You may be required to use the venue's exclusive vendors and may not like them or feel comfortable with them (or their pricing)

Getting Creative with Venues

Trying to break the reception hall mold? I commend you! But as you're searching "out of the box," remember that you do have to plan a successful party inside that box. Pick a location that is a unique environment but also (and more important) realistic in execution of what you can do. That said, here are some ideas for locale:

Waterside docks, piers,
   or buildings
Art galleries
Historical landmarks
Museums
Outdoor concert pavilions
Old theaters
Castles

Old estates or
   historic homes
Lofts
Parks
Nature conservancies
Aquariums, zoos
Botanical gardens

When considering a public venue, such as a museum or library, as a possible location, remember that in most cases it is used by the public during specific hours. Make sure you check the accessibility and availability for setting up your affair, as well as fees that may apply. Public venues are notorious for being grandiose and impressive, but also are notable for not being able to allow much setup time and for being costly, as you must likely compensate for possible loss of business, and other internal effects.

Working with Space

Remember how drab that big old gym looked at your high school dance? It wasn't just the bleachers and retired jerseys on the walls that gave it that look. It was also the size of the room. A party in tight quarters always looks better than a party scattered across too much space, so if you're out in the open, define the perimeter of your setting with decorations.

Tutera Tip: To add a little theatricality and an element of surprise, serve dinner in one area and dessert in another.

Tutera Tip: Don't be afraid to use air walls to minimize the size of a ballroom to fit your party. When the lights are dimmed, the smaller setting will be more intimate for your guests, and the air walls will go unnoticed.

Venue selection is important, so take your time. Your venue will be your home for over six hours . . . the most memorable six hours of your new lives together; choose it wisely and try not to settle! Once you do select that perfect space based on budget, locale, and style, you are ready to rock and roll.

Tutera Tip: Add the sales manager, director of catering, and/or maître d' to your "new best friend" list. The people in these positions are those who will execute your big day in your carefully selected venue. Communicate with them and make sure you are all on the same page with what you expect and what they can provide. In the end, you will be trusting them to run your show on the day of your wedding!

So you've picked your man. You've picked your date. And now you've picked your venue. What's next? Becoming the bride that will make that space not just a space, but a wedding.

Four

PERFECTLY POLISHED: ETIQUETTE FOR THE ELEGANT

You have spent so much time, money, and energy on making this day perfect that your behavior should reflect how much of a perfect bride you are to match! Proper grace is too often overlooked, and people make decisions that are inappropriate at their wedding (oh, the stories I have that no wedding words could describe and no bride should ever hear!). It's important to me to keep you from looking back six months, six years, or sixty years from now and saying, "What was I thinking? I should have thought and acted with a little more grace!" No retrospective pangs of regret for my brides; you're smart enough to take the precautions and learn the lessons now, while they can still help. In general, people have very short-term memories, but boy, oh boy, will they remember your wedding and all the decisions you made at it. Here are a few tips to keep everyone's memories (especially yours!) picture perfect.

I'M SMILING BECAUSE I HAVE TO RIGHT NOW: BEING A BRIDE WHO IS NICE AND CONSIDERATE TO ALL

Check any bridezilla tendencies at the door; this is the time to wear your most gracious smile and turn up the charm! While it is your wedding and you should have plenty to smile about, even the most put-together bride has a few moments where smiles don't come naturally (it's a natural part of any social engagement!). When those times come, be prepared. Think Princess Diana. Now, there's a woman who could put on the "nice" face even in the blinding lights of the paparazzi and amid royal pains. Make a list of the classiest women you have seen handle drama in the public eye. Channel a bit of their poise to help prepare you to handle anything and be the "hostess with the mostess." If they can do it, so can you!

I DO's:	I DON'Ts:
Princess Diana	Diana Ross
Ivana Trump	Paris Hilton
Julie Andrews	Britney Spears
Nicole Kidman	Lindsay Lohan
Grace Kelly	Kelly Osbourne
Marilyn Monroe	Pamela Anderson
Audrey Hepburn	Paula Abdul
Jackie Kennedy Onassis	Courtney Love

You will be "on stage" with people watching you every moment of the day of your wedding, so handle it calmly and with style. No temper tantrums, crying episodes, or fits of hysteria need apply! I know you are nervous, worried, and about to make a huge commitment, but stay calm and relaxed under all circumstances. You will come out on top. I promise! Make a vow to yourself to carry yourself with dignity. Avoid drinking too much alcohol. Curb the smoking (there is nothing more jarring than the sight of a bride in a beautiful dress with a cigarette in her mouth! If you need to do it—hide!). No screaming into your cell phone (in fact, no screaming at all!). If you are stressed, don't show it with anger or abruptness; meet it with a positive demeanor, no matter how difficult, how rude that guest was to wear white on your wedding day, or how late your florist is. What might be important to you now might not be important to you in twenty years when you are replaying your wedding video and see your outburst about an ice sculpture, and your kids are watching. You want people to remember you as pretty, polished, elated, thankful, fun, and in love, all day long. ("Stressed" has no place among those descriptives!) Take breaks if you need to. Slip away from the commotion or request some downtime to recharge. Don't be gone long enough to make you look like you could be the next runaway bride, but sparing a little time for yourself to simply relax and not be under the spotlight is a total "I do."

Tutera Tip: Select a friend or a bridesmaid to be your "buffer" all day. This person will fill the role of woman's wingman, the person who will be there to discreetly and politely excuse you (or prevent you) from awkward situations. She will be the dividing force and saving grace between you and your mother-in-law who wants to add her two cents too many times, an awkward guest you need to avoid, or a sobbing sister who wants to make the day about her. Choosing someone to help you navigate the obstacles before they create waves is the perfect antidote for smooth sailing.

YOUR A-LIST: CREATING YOUR GUEST LIST

With the what, where, when, and why covered, . . . it's time to solidify *who* will be joining you and witnessing your important moment and sharing in the postceremony fun. As you begin making your lists of lucky invitees, follow these guidelines of basic protocol.

Realistically question how many people you can invite, and how that should be divided between you and your groom. That will be answered by the subsequent question: Who's hosting the party? Traditionally, the bride's parents are hosting—if so, the bride's family gets to add more to their side of the guest list. If the groom's parents are hosting entirely or if they are splitting the bill, they have more say. (This has to be figured out in the beginning of the wedding to avoid drama down the planning road! Very important!) Keeping open communication with all parties is the biggest bit of advice I can offer to you.

Don't invite too many people! Know how many people are "too many." Let your venue determine how many guests it can hold, and then let your budget solidify how many people you can afford to have . . . or vice versa! Create a faux Rsvp list and go down your list of invitees to predict who will say yes, who will say no, and who is a maybe. This will help you determine how many guests you think you might get before you mail out your invites. Expect some declines by default. Approximately 15 percent will decline, but that is give or take, of course! If your wedding is on a holiday weekend, or if it is a destination wedding, the percentage of declines could be greater.

GET THE PARTY STARTED!: CHOOSING YOUR BRIDAL PARTY

Before you make the detailed list of who will be *at* your party, first make the list of who will be *in* your party: your bridal party, that is! When choosing your bridal attendants, think of who will be there for you if you and your husband ever need help; if you encounter difficulties in your marriage, who will support your relationship most?

Those are the people who make great bridesmaids and groomsmen. You will be casting your supporting roles of:

- Maid/Matron of Honor
- Bridesmaids
- Junior Bridesmaid(s)
- Flower Girl(s)
- Mothers of the Bride/Groom
- Grandmothers
- Best Man
- Groomsmen
- Ring Bearer
- Fathers of the Bride/Groom
- Grandfathers
- Readers
- Ushers
- Hostesses/Points of Contact/Helpers
- Lady/Gentleman-in-Waiting (This is a hired position)

YOUR DEFINING MOMENT: A BRIDAL ATTENDANTS GLOSSARY

Hostess. Can greet guests, hand out programs and toss items, and/or help direct guests where to go. A perfect role for a young lady or gentleman.

Ushers. Gentlemen (not in the bridal party) who will escort the women to their seats at the ceremony.

Readers. Friends or family members chosen to read passages (often religious) during the service. Could be in the bridal party.

Points of Contact. People in charge of answering questions, and directing guests with where to go or what to do (thereby freeing up the bride, groom, and bridal party).

Ladies/Gentlemen-in-waiting. In historic times, a lady-in-waiting was appointed to serve or attend a queen, princess, or royal duchess (I think you see where I'm going with this). A lady-in-waiting for you, on your day of royal pampering, should be a hired role due to the nature of the work, which is to assist you with your every whim. From helping you get dressed to keeping you organized, to running emergency errands, your lady-in-waiting is there to get you through the day while your maid/matron of honor and bridesmaids are preparing for your ceremony.

Are you having any pets in the wedding? I have dressed up dogs to match the bride and groom, and cats to be the ring bearer. If you choose to include your furry friends, also assign a "handler" (a friend or someone who is familiar with your animal) to guide them in the ceremony.

Tutera Tip: You don't have to match your number of bridesmaids with the number of groomsmen. Brides are often under the impression that there needs to be an even number of each side of the bridal party—not true!

The Crème de la Crème

I have seen a bridal party of one person, where the matron of honor was the bride's mom. I've seen a bridal party of fifty-seven people (I kid you not), parading down the aisle and making the processional more like a three-ring circus than a wedding. (They were wrapped around the church! You want your party to "stand up" at the wedding, not crowd around!) If you're in the selection process, keep in mind that the more bridesmaids you have, the more work (and hand-holding) it will take to get everyone on the same page. While it may be tempting to have lots of friends don the pretty matching dresses and vests, think seriously about it: Even if you have the most obedient and loving supporting cast, you must still figure out fashion, transportation, timing, and a lot of logistics that are ultimately your responsibility. Each of these attendants will need your supervision to ensure they have the right dress (and that they can pay for it), as well as the right shoes and accessories; that they know the timeline and when to arrive for hair and makeup appointments; that they can attend the rehearsal dinner; that they have transportation; that they are there on time for that transportation. . . . You might think you want nine bridal attendants, but remember that you would have to do a lot more work as a bride than if you were to have just three. It could be fun . . . but it might not be as easy as it seems. (I once had a bride who had so many bridesmaids and got so stressed out she ended up firing one—and another quit! And while boys will be boys and possibly not get mixed up in "this vest makes me look fat" commentary, they have just as many tasks and responsibilities to abide by as well.) You don't want to be surrounded by any environments that breed negative energy, so make it easy for yourself and keep it manageable, taking on only as much as you and your groom truly can handle. Asking a bridesmaid to be a bridesmaid is a big responsibility for both you and her—you need to choose someone whom you trust as well as someone who is willing to spearhead all the tasks that go along with the role. They can't just show up one day and be in the wedding—there are engagement parties, wedding showers, bachelor and bachelorette parties, bridesmaids' teas, spa parties, rehearsals and rehearsal dinners, and *then*, after all that, is an even bigger deal: your wedding day. It's a lot of responsibility to ask someone to be in your bridal party. It takes time, money, commitment, and, most important, love.

Now is not the time to make any decisions you will regret. If you're down to the wire, deciding between a friend and a relative, always keep in mind the inclusion of new members of your family. You're not just marrying the man—you're marrying his family (and boy, oh boy, if that isn't one of the first lessons of marriage, I don't know what is!). If you are choosing between someone you knew in college and a new sibling-in-law, remember that a part of your new life as a spouse-to-be is to put family first—even if it is his. Your friends may not be there forever, but your sister-in-law will be. (This is a decision you'll have to live with for the rest of your life!) So if you are pressured to choose a sister-in-law or family member (even if you would rather not), bend. You'll thank me later when she's not giving you *the look* across the Thanksgiving dinner table, still upset that you did not let her wear the lavender dress and fluff your train. And your friend will still be at your wedding—give her priority seating and invite her to the bachelorette party to ensure she is there for all the right memories. That your first priority is your new family is something everyone will understand.

PLAYING THE PART: THE ROLE OF THE BRIDE AND GROOM

The day is all about you, of course, but there are just a few special wedding responsibilities you and your groom have to your guests. While your day should never be consumed by running around and making sure your guests are having a good time at every moment, it's important that you take time and make efforts to let them know that you care they are present. Receiving lines, toasts, and the appropriate amount of greeting and mingling make up the perfect combination of efforts to prove to your guests that you and your groom are the perfect hosts.

Tutera Tip: On the day of your wedding, stay side by side with your new husband at every moment. People want and need to see you two together following a ceremony honoring your union and throughout the entire celebration.

BEING WELL RECEIVED
AT YOUR RECEPTION

Wedding receptions are said to be derived from royal feasts. The concept of a dinner with king- and queenlike figures presiding over an abundance of food and guests, with entertainment provided, is right out of a Shakespearean play (but one in which everyone lives happily ever after). While I do not expect you to adopt all the "thee's" and "thy's" and "doths" of that time period, I do think there is something of that period's regality and proper behavior to be learned and practiced on this, the glorious day of thy wedding (I couldn't resist).

I DO's for Reception Bridal Behavior

* Do remember your manners as you dine! Everyone will be looking at you at some point, just out of curiosity to see what you are doing. Eyes are *always* on the bride. So please. Use your napkin. Don't talk with your mouth open. Don't stab your food. Don't eat with your fingers. But you already know all these things, I hope!

* Drink minimally. Even though you are so overjoyed, your reception is still not the ideal time to swing from the chandeliers! (*That* was what your bachelorette party was for.) I once had a beautiful bride who consumed so much alcohol that she jumped on a stage and modeled her ten-thousand-dollar wedding gown as though she was reliving her college days at a fraternity party. In a few years, she will wish she had been more careful with every moment of the day she and her groom will remember for the rest of their lives together (and then some; I think that bridal catwalk strut will live on in infamy).

* This is the time to consistently mingle and make sure everyone at your party sees you and your groom. Go table to table, engage in conversations, and share only kind words.

- While you mingle at your reception, take a moment to eat. Knowing you will be both excited and busy and your appetite may be minimal, eat breakfast the morning of your wedding and eat throughout the day to avoid fatigue and light-headedness.
- Have a guest book out for your guests to sign and write you their good wishes.

I DON'Ts for Reception Bridal Behavior

- Please don't take your shoes off. You're not at home kicking back and watching TV. You should feel comfortable at your own wedding, but not *that* comfortable!
- Gentlemen should not take off their jackets (especially the groom), even if the room is warm. Out of respect for the attire and formality of the wedding, wait until the main entrée is cleared.
- No hiking up your dress to bump and grind on the dance floor! Please no shake-your-moneymaker moves or "wedding night previews" for your guests (you paid for entertainment, so you do not have to be it).
- Don't drink beer out of the bottle or smoke cigarettes where your guests can see you.
- Don't lose your bouquet. Have a bridesmaid keep an eye on it for you as well.
- Keep your language as pretty as you look! On your wedding day, leave the swearing to the sailors.
- Don't spend too much time with one group of people at your wedding reception (even though you may have your favorites). Be the perfect host by mingling and spending time and making memories with everyone.
- Don't *lick the cake knife* after you cut your beautiful wedding cake. I've seen it done . . . and it's just not right. (I sometimes have nightmares of brides doing it as I dive to-

ward them in slow motion to grab the knife out of their hand.)

- Don't break away from your groom! Now isn't the time for him to be at the bar with his buddies and for you to be cutting it up on the dance floor with your best girl-friends. These are your first married moments, and people want to see you together (and you should want to be to-gether!).

OH, YOU SHOULDN'T HAVE!: REGISTRY AND GIFTS

Creating your registry is like making an electronically organized adult holiday wish list. This "task" should actually be quite fun for you both. When else will you ever get to shop for yourself, pick out exactly what you want, know you will receive it, and—oh yes!—not pay for anything? (That's what I thought! You're excited now!)

Though this is a very thrilling moment, starry-eyed couples with dreams of decorating their ideal home and furnishing their kitchens and dens with everything in every aisle may get carried away, so don't go too crazy! Now is the time to pick and choose whatever your heart desires, but remember that registries exist to help you get your new home started. This is the main push you get from the world to help you begin in your "real" life. Choose things like bedding, kitchen-ware, table-top items (casual, formal, and everyday), luggage, bath-room needs, and a few fantasy gifts (yes, yes, the big-screen TV and the crystal vase).

Tutera Tip: With china, register for a minimum of twelve settings so you have enough to entertain for the holidays. A few years down the road, you may be hosting Thanksgiving for the family, or even your kids.

While registries used to be just for china, they can include almost anything these days . . . but restrain yourself from registering for anything too bizarre or too trite. For instance, nothing should be chosen from the candy aisle. Please do not register for shampoo. Refrain from pointing that scanner at anything too personal on your wish list; you can go buy groceries and toiletries anytime! Take my advice: Register for the pepper grinder. You'll thank me later.

Register in at least two places (the more well known, the better. If you like, pick a specialty store for a third). Also, ensure that you ask for items of all different prices. Your grandparents might splurge for the entire china set, while your college roommate may not be able to make it to the wedding but will still want to buy something (not as grand) to help you on your way. Choose some small items to act as "filler" pieces for people who will buy you groupings of gifts or for those looking for the right engagement or shower gift. Last, choose some expensive pieces so that if a group of friends want to chip in for something larger, they have the option.

Registering for gifts should be a fun experience for you and your groom. Make it a date, followed by a nice dinner to reward yourselves for accomplishing it! I suggest taking a day with your fiancé and shopping 'til you drop. Make lists at each retailer, and come with stamina (remember, girls, he's a man and does not have years of marathon shopping experience like you do). Allow him to pick out his fair share of items, including some things just for him. While his buddies might pool together to buy him that big-screen TV thinking of game night, imagine how Humphrey Bogart will look on a big screen that large when you watch *Casablanca* after they're done.

Registries are primarily designed for convenience. With shopping online so accessible, everyone involved in the registry process can participate efficiently and effectively (including you who are choosing gifts, your guests who are purchasing them, and your retailers who are supplying them).

For the Internet-savvy, the time-crunched, the elders who cannot make shopping runs, and travelers who may not have your stores in their hometowns, online registries are a must.

Back in the day (circa 1995), guests were expected to go to the stores where you were registered and choose what you wanted from a paper list. People of past generations may feel traditionally inclined to still do this. If you have some traditionalists among your guests, think of what stores are around them as well as around you.

How to Share Your Registry with Others

Registry information should never ever be included on or with your invite (you are asking guests to celebrate your love, not buy you gifts!). Instead, personal wedding Web sites are the best nonintrusive way to share where you're registered. The wedding shower invite is also an appropriate place to slip in a modest piece of paper with the information, and never bypass the old standby, word of mouth—inform your bridal party and your parents where you are registered so they can pass it along if anyone asks (and they will!).

Tutera Tip: Register early! Engagement gifts, shower gifts, and your wedding gifts should all come from your master registries. It's much easier this way for you and your guests, as the presents start coming in almost as soon as you say "I will!"

As much as you need a money tree in the backyard of your newly-wed home, a proper way to ask for cash unfortunately does not exist. Word of mouth is the only polite way to divulge this information. That said, there is nothing wrong with having a registry at a store or two, and prepping your bridal party with some information about your preferences for green instead of crystal, silver, or china. If your parents and bridal party are able to share with inquiring guests a line like "I think they would benefit from money to start their new home the most," that is a perfect way to get the point across without having sticky fingers!

On the day of your wedding, you can expect money in envelopes and some gifts to take home. Prepare someone—a bridal party member or parent—to be the designated gift-taker-homer. Set up a gift table in your foyer or an out-of-the-way yet visible location to receive what people may bring by hand.

Gifts on your registry will start to come in the moment you post the links to the wine rack and the dishtowels. Connect an address to your registry where you can receive gifts and shipments before and after your nuptials. If you are moving into a home together postwedding, choose a parent's address to receive shipments to avoid having to forward your gifts or having them get lost in transit. Keep an address on your personal Web site as well; for up to one year postwedding, it is still appropriate for people to send you wedding gifts (though they will most likely not be the ones on your registry, as those get snapped up quickly).

Tutera Tip: Be gracious when you receive gifts that are not on your registry. Everyone forgets that there was a time registries did not even exist. To this day, though they are commonplace, registries are simply a method of convenience rather than a gift-giving obligation.

Honeymoon registries are becoming more and more popular, and while I am not a big advocate of them (as registries are intended to start your home, and honeymoons are very personal) I do understand how a little boost can upgrade your whole vacation. Your honeymoon is a very intimate activity. It's one of the *first* things you should plan as husband and wife together, and a good tone is set for your life when the first thing you pay for as a couple is a romantic escape. Alas, this is a personal decision, so whichever way you decide, make sure your guests who want to contribute to your new home can do so and that your honeymoon maintains intimacy (even in the planning) for you and your new husband.

FROM ME TO YOU: WHEN TO GIFT GUESTS

For guests who have traveled from afar or who are staying in one of the main hotels, it's such a hospitable gesture to welcome them, as the bride and groom, with a note and a small token of appreciation for their efforts in making it to your wedding. Welcome baskets and small gifts in your guests' hotel rooms will bring a smile to their faces and make them glad they made the trip before your wedding has even begun.

Arrival Gifts

In a basket, include snacks (bottled water, granola bars, candy) and fact sheets about the surroundings with some brochures of things to do. Or tie a welcome note (from both you and the groom) to a small gift local to the area to give your guests a "taste" of their new locale. Guests traveling to a wedding in Vermont could receive maple-flavored candies, and a bride in Texas might give out bottles of the best local barbeque sauce. A small assortment of chocolates from the town's best candy store, or tickets to a nearby activity or tour are all great ways to thank visitors for coming such a long way to see you.

Departure Gifts

At the end of your wedding day, guests staying overnight will want to climb into a perfect bed. Have a note with a favor (a piece of candy or a sprig of lavender) placed on their pillows, wishing them sweet dreams from the bride and groom.

YOUR SUPPORTING CAST: ATTENDANT GIFTS

There are some very special "guests" you and your groom need to thank after your wedding. For you, they were your official ladies-in-waiting. Your best girlfriends. Your sisters, your favorite people, and—most likely—some very deserving gals for helping you (if they were good bridesmaids) get to this day and down the aisle. Most important, they are your friends. When choosing them, you asked yourself who would support you both as a couple, should you ever need guidance. For all of this (not to mention for all the trips to the seamstress, for picking up your bouquets, for tasting every flavor of cake, and for helping you choose between magenta and crimson), they deserve your thanks.

You can thank your bridesmaids in many ways, either before or after the wedding. The day before, treat them to a prewedding spa day (where it's all about *them* for a moment!). It is customary to give each a special gift (with a little something extra for your maid/matron of honor). From jewelry to handbags to individual gifts that match their personalities, whatever you choose, this task should be an easy and fun one for the bride; the person who knows them best is you!

Tutera Tip: Sisters of the groom or relatives in your bridal party you may not know as well as your best girls should still be thanked for standing up with you. Do your best to find out their likes and dislikes to get them a thoughtful tribute for their participation.

BRIDESMAID GIFT IDEAS
- Gift certificates for spa treatments or shopping sprees
- Tote bags of goodies: nail polishes, subscriptions to magazines, chocolates, earrings, pretty gloves, perfumes
- Scarves

- Monogrammed items: silver photo frames, compact mirrors
- Personalized stationery and pens
- Handbags or wallets
- Jewelry pieces or jewelry boxes
- Travel accessories
- Crystal vanity sets
- Candles and lotions
- Fine wines or flavored liqueurs

Don't forget the men! Your groom will need to select gifts to thank his league of extraordinary gentlemen who did the same for him.

GROOMSMEN GIFT IDEAS

- Silver monogrammed gifts such as money clips
- Pocket watches
- Leather wallets
- Shaving kits
- Poker sets and playing cards
- Boxes of cigars
- Subscriptions to magazines
- Monogrammed pens
- Fine scotches or liquors
- Barbeque grill sets (did you know you can brand a steak with your initials?)
- Cuff links and studs
- Ties
- Sunglasses
- Sports and golf memberships or accessories

And don't forget age-appropriate gifts for your flower girl and ring bearer. For a young lady, a special piece of jewelry is a perfect way to make her feel like a grown-up for participating in your grown-up ceremony. For the ring bearer, I've seen it all, from a remote-control boat to a sterling-silver yo-yo to a special edition of a comic book. The more personal, even with kids, the better.

The right etiquette sends a consistent message from you to your guests and to all who watch you on the day of your wedding: You are poised, graceful, mature, polite, and fit to be both a bride and a hostess, the ultimate combination for running a perfectly polished wedding.

Five

YOU'RE INVITED!: INVITES AND PRINTED MATERIALS

We squeal on cue at our best friend's engagement ring and talk about the big day with just the right sense of awe, but if you hear someone squeal after finding a big ivory envelope with calligraphy on it amid the bills and coupons, sometimes it's not simply out of joy, but also out of the imminent chores that go with attending another wedding . . . another weekend to take off . . . travel plans to afford . . . another registry gift to buy. . . . What happened to the delight of being invited and attending a wedding?

When you're creating invitations, don't think of them just from the bridal perspective: Imagine what it will be like for your guests to actually be receiving them. When your guests receive the invitation to your wedding, it should set a tone of excitement for the entire affair. The outside of the envelope, the stamps, the layout of the invitation, and the font—all the details count. A great invitation creates curiosity and intrigue. If you want to really grab the attention of your guests, design an invitation that guarantees the impression that yours is a wedding not to be missed.

I've had a lot of fun with clients who were willing to get creative and send out an invitation that stretched the imagination. Your printed materials are more than just paper goods: They are the first chapter of the story of your wedding day—the cover, even! They can be a way to further express your style, and carry on the story of your wedding. For every event, people look toward the reading material they are given to gather information, and your wedding is no different! It all sets the tone, the style, and the vibe of your celebrations. Wedding printed materials are your voice to your guests throughout the party, from save the dates you send out hoping guests will come, to the thank-you cards that show your gratitude, and all the in-betweens.

PRINTED MATERIALS
- Save the dates
- Invitations: Rsvp cards, directions, envelopes
- Programs
- Escort cards
- Place cards
- Table numbers
- Cocktail menus
- Menu cards
- Favor notes

PRINTED GOODS THAT DO NOT NECESSARILY NEED TO MATCH IN STYLE
- Thank-you notes
- Bachelorette/bachelor party invites
- Wedding shower invites
- Rehearsal dinner invites

I think it's a fabulous touch to have your materials correlate with one another. I instruct my brides to do this to maintain a certain continuity throughout their weddings, to project an all-encompassing feeling around the various components of their celebration—in short, your printed materials can really tie it all in together.

Once you've chosen the colors you'd like to use, play around with selecting a font to fit your personalities and the theme of your wedding. If you're going chic and funky, choose a font that looks modern, hip, and edgy. A traditional, classic wedding? Then choose a beautiful script! The font alone can get guests in the right frame of mind for what style of party to expect and how formal an event to prepare for.

A logo that can be used on your materials will be the perfect last touch. This has the same psychological basis as a company using a logo to brand itself—to take its formality up a notch and to help people identify with what is going on overall. Many brides of mine choose a beautifully designed monogram. For others, their logo might be a flower reminiscent of their surroundings, or a graphic that denotes something about their personalities—for a couple that actually met on the cross streets of Fifty-sixth and Park, their logo design was a fun combination of both street names that they used throughout their wedding, placing it on the top of the program, on the favor tags, and even monogrammed onto fleece blankets for their guests to keep warm at a chilly autumn ceremony. For a couple with an Irish wedding, I created a special crest for them that appeared on their menu cards, their escort cards, and even in their topiaries.

Creating your logo should be a fun project for you and your groom, and will be something you can treasure for the rest of your lives together. Your symbol can be as creative or as formal as you like—it's a great way to play around with fonts and text, with graphic designs and colors, to create something that guests can visually identify with, that can bring them from one part of your wedding to the next mentally (and logistically: They can use it as a sign they are in the right place!). This is a task your invitation company can greatly assist you with.

With your colors, your font, and your logo ready to go, you are ready to tackle all your printed materials with style, ease, and—hopefully—fun!

CREATING A BUZZ: SAVE THE DATES

Save the dates should be a fun, low-stress way to spread the news that you're officially getting married! Send out save-the-date cards six to eight months before your wedding—eight months in advance is best if many of your guests will be traveling from out of town and need to make arrangements. . . . And if it's on a holiday weekend or at a destination, save the dates are a must!

Having save the dates that match the invitation to follow is my favorite way to go; however, it is not necessary. Since your primary goal is to spread the message (and soon), you either may not have the invites planned yet or you may want this to be an opportunity to have some fun with telling everyone your news! With save the dates, you have some room to play. You can also design the save the date to tie in with your venue, if you know where it is. The information you need on the save the dates is your names, the fact that you're getting married, the date and the city in which your wedding will take place (so guests can plan), and that there will be a formal invitation to follow.

Save the Date!
Ronald Forbes and Rebecca Hampton
are getting married!
Saturday, April 17, 2010
Seattle, Washington
Formal Invitation to Follow

Remember, a save-the-date card is like a preinvitation—once you send it to a person, by the standards of etiquette you have invited them to the wedding and must send them an invitation. The most terrible thing you can do is send a save the date to someone and revoke it, leading to an awkward conversation about why they did not get a real invitation! All that said, don't skip sending save the dates overall; they're in your best interest for planning purposes. The benefit for you? You can have the turnout you want and also get a feel for how many people will (and will not) attend. As you'll be dealing with numbers (remember how many of your budget predictions depend on your guest count?), this is helpful information to gauge as early as possible.

I DO's of Save-the-Date Cards

* Be creative and stylish with your save the dates! For a formal wedding, it's customary to send a layered card matching a formal invite in an envelope, but for more "fun" weddings (e.g., an outdoor fall wedding in a tent), send a save the date on a pretty leaf in a box from a craft store. Going somewhere? For destination weddings, have postcards sent from the location saying "Can't wait to see you here on December 14 for our special day!" For a beach wedding, send a message in a bottle with sand, gems, pearls, and a rolled-up note with your information.

* Make sure to send save the dates if you are having a destination wedding or a wedding that takes place on a holiday weekend (or a popular travel time—like around Christmas or Thanksgiving); they are a must to let your guests know far enough in advance to avoid conflicting plans.

* Even if a recipient of your save-the-date card lets you know they cannot attend before the invites are officially sent, send them one anyway. (Hey, you may get a gift or at least a nice card out of it, too.)

I DON'Ts for Save-the-Date Cards

- Evites (as trendy as they are) or e-mails do not count as save the dates. Don't send save the dates (or, of course, your formal wedding invitations) through the Internet—always send them through the postal service.
- Don't forget to send save the dates to even the VIPs: your bridal party and groomsmen, and even your parents! Just because they are involved doesn't mean they shouldn't feel like valued guests, too!
- If you are inviting someone to bring a guest with them, don't forget to address the save the date to that person "and guest." Decide in advance who you're inviting with and without a guest to avoid confusion later on.

Should My Guest Bring a Guest?

When making your guest list, you must decide whether single friends and family members will be invited with a guest. I am often asked what is correct regarding this issue! I generally encourage brides to invite singles to bring guests unless it becomes a budgetary issue or physical space is limited for your event. If you need to make some choices, here are my "I Do's" and "I Don'ts" for plus-ones.

LET THEM INVITE A GUEST IF

- Your guest is a close relative
- Your guest is a friend and you've met their girl/boyfriend a few times
- Your guest is a bridal party member
- You are concerned about your guest feeling comfortable and mingling and you think they would be happier with company

DON'T LET THEM INVITE A GUEST IF

- Your guest just started dating someone
- You have never met your guest's significant other

Tutera Tip: If you are close with your guest, there is nothing wrong with asking them how they feel about bringing (or not bringing) a guest.

Your save the dates are the first piece of "literature" your guests will receive about your wedding, so it's important that you demonstrate through them how much you would love for your guests to be there. (Though it's true that nothing has the same impact as the fabulous invitation that you will follow it up with!) Which leads us to . . .

YOU ARE CORDIALLY INVITED: INVITATIONS

Your invitation is where you really make a statement about your event! Send invites out about two to three months before the wedding date, and have fun with creating them. Invitations are glimpses into your party, and are the first impressions your guests get before attending. Set the tone and the style, and include all the pertinent information.

The invitation itself should include:

- Your names
- Who is hosting
- Date and time
- Ceremony location
- "Reception to Follow"
- A separate reception card with location and directions
- Rsvp date with response card and self-addressed stamped envelope
- Attire
- Your return address on the mailing envelope

The order and the wording is where you and your invitation designer can take creative liberty to make it match your wedding style. For example:

FORMAL

Mr. and Mrs. Michael Saxton
request the honor of your presence
at the marriage of their daughter
Sarah May

to

Mr. Sumeet Bagai
on Saturday, the ninth of March
two thousand eleven
at half past six o'clock in the evening
The Plaza Hotel
Fifth Avenue
New York, New York
Reception immediately following
Black Tie

INFORMAL

With Joy in Our Hearts,
Sarah Saxton

and

Sumeet Bagai
request the pleasure of your presence
at their wedding celebration
Saturday, the ninth of March
two thousand and eleven
six o'clock in the evening
The Maritime
New York, New York
Reception immediately following
Black Tie Optional

All Dressed Up with Somewhere to Go: Attire

Whether your wedding is formal or casual, always state the dress attire on the invite. Take the guesswork out for your guests and also create uniformity to complete the look of your party. When you state what the attire is, it should be simple and clear (you don't want everyone calling and e-mailing you questions about what to wear!). Steer clear from attire phrases that leave room for interpretation (i.e., Festive Attire, Creative Attire, Creative Tie, Casual Attire, Downtown Chic . . .). Stick to the traditional attire options below:

- Black Tie
- Black Tie Optional
- White Tie
- Evening Attire
- Cocktail Attire
- All-White Attire

Now that you've tackled the main portion of your invite, be sure to include the rest of the pieces and inserts that make an invitation complete. You will need to include:

- An Rsvp/reply card.
- A stamped reply-card envelope, preaddressed to the parents of the bride, the wedding host, the bride herself, or someone who will be receiving and tallying guest count.
- A direction card of how guests can find your ceremony and reception location. Include directions from the nearest airport and train stations, or from major nearby hotels. Offer a variety of ways to access your venues.
- A reception card, if your ceremony and reception are in two different locations. Insert a separate card explaining and directing guests to your party location. Remember, the formal invite is just the invite to your ceremony with "Reception to

Follow," which leads your guests to expect and need more information.

- A list of nearby hotels for travelers and guests unfamiliar with the area, to help them make arrangements. Speak with the nearby hotels to set up "room blocks" with special rates for your guests. (When a hotel knows your wedding will bring in a good deal of business, they may give you a discounted rate per room and ensure the rooms are near each other.)
- A brief itinerary if your wedding is a multiday affair.

Tutera Tip: For the rehearsal dinner, when asking guests to Rsvp, ask them to send you a photo of you and your groom to let you know he (or she) will be attending your party. By putting each photo in a beautiful frame, you can create fun decor.

Style and Class: Invitation Sass

How many times have you decided to buy a product in the store because it was in attractive packaging? (Be honest . . . there is a reason we naturally gravitate toward attractive advertisements!) Presentation and the hint of what's to come is such a driving force in the marketing industry; it's undeniable that people are lured into participating because good presentation instills a sense of excitement into them.

The act of encouraging people to attend your wedding operates on the same psychological principles, which is why the invitation is so important. Let's drum up the excitement through your first contact with them!

YOUR DEFINING MOMENT: AN INVITATION LAYOUT GLOSSARY

Traditional Panel Card. A single card that slides directly into a mailing envelope.

Pocket Fold. An invite card that is inserted within a larger component resembling a folder. Guests slide out the invitation card to reveal the information regarding your wedding.

Insert Sides. Often horizontal, a "booklet cover" that opens to reveal information inserted on both sides, layered so guests can easily identify which cards contain which information.

Self-Mailer. A wedding invitation that does not need a separate envelope. Your invitation information is printed on a paper insert that sits inside the "mailer," a paper in a strategic shape that, when folded, closes itself. A sticker or tie secures the self-mailer in place.

Box. An invitation within a box rather than a paper envelope. Box invitations vary greatly based on style, fabric, and materials used. Commonly, a ribbon ties the box lid shut, and upon opening the lid, the recipient discovers the invitation inside atop decorative filling.

Tutera Tip: Show your love for the earth as well as for each other. Use recycled invitation paper to save the environment while making a great statement that you are a considerate and conscious bride.

Choosing a style for your invitation allows you as the host to be as formal or creative as you want with your wedding from your earliest stage. I have included templates for a standard formal invitation (Classic Black Tie), a traditional invitation with a twist (Vintage Hollywood), an informal wedding (Casual Autumn), a modern wedding, and a destination beach wedding. Easy to re-create or adapt to your own specific style, you will find that each template includes suggestions for the colors, ink, envelope, and font.

Traditional and Formal Invites

A formal wedding calls for a formal invitation that is printed, plain, and elegant. Traditional wording in a simple script on a panel card can be accented with sedate trim, a beautiful monogram, and sophisticated (not edgy) colors. I suggest using a heavy-stock paper in cream or white. The most formal of invitations is considered to be an enveloped invitation inserted within a larger addressed mailing envelope. (Technically, you are sending two envelopes per set.) The inner envelope should have the guest's name written in calligraphy. Talk about a formal delivery!

CLASSIC BLACK-TIE FORMAL WEDDING TEMPLATE
Invite: Cream, trimmed in gold border
Ink: Black
Inside envelope lining: Cream
Font: Edwardian Script

Traditional with a twist

Invites to your wedding do not necessarily have to be traditional in order for people to value it as a "serious" wedding. Show that your formal wedding is happening with a bit of unique pizzazz (but be wary of coming across as "themed" or "cheesy"). One of my favorite styles that keeps the wedding formal while also adding some personality is "Vintage Hollywood." The glitz, the glamour, and the high style in itself!

VINTAGE HOLLYWOOD TEMPLATE
Invite: White
Ink: Black
Accents: Shades of pink with glitzy accessories (crystals, feathers, pearls)
Inside envelope lining: Black or pearl/opal
Font: COPPERPLATE GOTHIC

Nontraditional and Casual

If your wedding goes against the grain and is all about kicking back and having a good time, let that show and have a good time designing your invite. Keep the color, logo, and font streamlined; those elements will all keep you looking well put together as a host.

CASUAL AUTUMN WEDDING TEMPLATE

Invite: Brown

Ink: Copper

Accents: Sunset colors

Inside envelope lining: plaid

Font: Freestyle Script

Chic and Modern

A modern invitation reflects your wedding style. Draw upon your venue, time of year, and your personality to make your invitations more than just words on paper. With sleek lines, shiny inks, and glossy textures, a formal invitation can turn into a forward-thinking formal invitation with a contemporary feel.

MODERN WEDDING TEMPLATE

Invite: Lucite or glossy white

Ink: Pewter or black

Accents: Sparkle, crystals

Inside envelope lining: Pewter or high-gloss white

Font: Whitney

Destination Wedding

Because of the special nature of these weddings, you can easily go formal or casual. For a beach wedding, send a message in a bottle in lieu of an invitation. Handwrite an invitation in black ink on ivory paper, roll it into a tube, and tie it with a piece of twine. Funnel the scrolled invitation into an empty clear bottle, and add small seashells, crystals, sand, and pearls. Cork or screw the top back on and if possible, hand-deliver to the doorsteps of your fellow vacationers.

BEACH WEDDING TEMPLATE

Invite: White

Ink: Green or blue (oceanic colors)

Accent: Beige rattan

Inside envelope lining: green or blue

Font: Bradley Hand ITC

YOUR DEFINING MOMENT: A FONT EMBELLISHMENT GLOSSARY

Engraving. Lettering or designs are impressed or cut into paper (most expensive).

Embossing. Lettering or designs are pressed into paper, and then given a raised, textured finish.

Raised Ink. Printed sheets are treated with a fine layer of colored powder that attaches to wet ink and is then hardened. An option similar to but more economical than embossing.

Formal Calligraphy. There are two types of calligraphy to choose from when addressing envelopes for your invitation. The first type is pen-and-ink calligraphy, which is printed by hand. The second type is done by computers and replicates the look of handwritten calligraphy. This method is not necessarily less expensive and can sometimes look as if it was done mechanically, thus losing the effect of hand-printed calligraphy. Both can be done in a color to match the invite ink and accent colors. Always ask to see samples of the calligrapher's work.

Tutera Tip: The more elaborate your invitation, the more time you should allow for receiving and reviewing proofs from your printer. If your invite company charges you per proof, ask if that cost can be applied toward your overall bill.

Addressing the Invites

When addressing envelopes, be as specific as possible. If you have accommodated for the guest to bring a date, list your guest's name and "and guest." If your guest has a steady significant other, you may choose to list the name of that person. If he or she has a fiancé, it is considered rude not to list the other person by name and you must invite them both. The same is true if a person is married: You need to invite the spouse even if you do not know him or her. Below are some ways to list couples:

EXAMPLE 1

Mr. and Mrs. James Hammond

Or

Mr. James Hammond

Mrs. Sara Hammond

Or

James and Sara Hammond

EXAMPLE 2

Dr. and Mrs. Austin Trotter

Or

Dr. Austin Trotter

Mrs. Kristi Trotter

Or

Austin and Kristi Trotter

EXAMPLE 3

Ms. Elizabeth Chu and Guest

Or

Ms. Elizabeth Chu

and

Guest

Lutera Tip: Have extra blank escort cards, menu cards, place cards, and the right calligraphy pen on hand the day of for last-minute changes. Order twenty-five extra invite sets for mistakes,

last-minute add-ons, new friends, and just to have as
keepsakes.

Mailing your invitations through the regular post-office system will put black marks from the machinery on the invitation. For a cleaner, "old-fashioned" formal look, take your invites to the post office to be hand-cancelled: They will be hand-stamped for a prettier final look that your guests will see when they arrive.

Make a special area of your house (with two baskets or letter holders) designated for your wedding work. Put declines in one pile and acceptances in the other so you can gauge what your guest count looks like at all times as you talk with your vendors; this is always good information to know. (Or, if you're one of the lucky brides who have someone like a bridesmaid or a parent taking care of your invite Rsvps, defer this task to them!) Transfer your yeses and nos into a working computer document where you can then track gifts, thank-you notes, and more throughout your wedding process.

Tutera Tip: Don't forget to hang on to your list of addresses to make your life easier when you write thank-you notes—you'll have it all ready to go again!

WHAT DO WE DO NOW?: ITINERARIES

If your wedding has multiple components to it, having an itinerary is helpful to inquiring guests and keeps you and your bridal party from having to continuously explain to others what the plans are. If your wedding is a destination celebration, takes place over a series of days, or you have many out-of-town guests, an itinerary will be key in relaying transportation and timing information to your guests.

With itineraries, it's all about the flow of events and seamless transitions. Simply put, your guests need to know what time they need to be where, how to get from here to there, and what to do in between events.

When making your itinerary, begin with the schedule of main events: a welcome dinner, the rehearsal dinner, the wedding, the cocktail hour, the reception, and a farewell brunch. Then fill in any other group or optional activities that have a time slot. Leave plenty of time for guests to be late, lost, or confused, so they get to where they are going on time.

Once you have the main events, list transportation details as clearly and as detailed as possible on the itinerary, so guests can easily find travel accommodations to each activity or event. Information about bus pickups and drop-offs and hotel shuttles or car services belongs here. Include not only what time the transportation leaves, but what time guests are requested to be at the meeting point to catch it.

Tutera Tip: Find the right balance of scheduling your guests' time. Don't leave them without options and things to do, but also don't overload your guests with too many scheduled activities. Downtime for guests to relax and spend time with each other is helpful to keep them happy (and they will love you even more if you don't drag them everywhere!).

For out-of-town guests, it is kind to include a list of local activities and visitors' attractions that guests can partake in on their own time before and/or after your wedding. Include movie theaters, restaurants, museums, shopping, and historical landmarks along with phone numbers, addresses, Web sites, and brochures. A special touch is to include a contact in the bridal party for guests to call if they have any questions or need recommendations.

Tutera Tip: As the bride and groom, clue your guests in on some of your favorite spots around the town. Provide a map with pinpoints to note places like the restaurant you met in and your favorite

date spot. Adding a touch of your personality acquaints them
with your city and further shares the story of your love.

There will likely be more activities (whether planned by the resort or offered by your own arrangements) during a destination wedding than at traditional weddings. The dress code should be indicated in accordance with each activity so guests know what to pack and how to dress the part!

Tutera Tip: While you are scheduling, remember to enjoy yourself! Never take things too seriously. An aura of something unexpected should be incorporated in all parties. It allows guests to wonder about what might be around the corner, creating an anticipation of surprise.

THE RUN OF SHOW: PROGRAMS

Much like the wedding invitations, if you are using ceremony programs, have them reflect the style of your wedding. Many programs can be made of the same materials and with the same designs as the invitations, which adds a nice continuity.

If you can repeat the design, font, and style, then let your imagination take flight with how to present your program. If it's a formal event, it's very appropriate to have a neat, sophisticated program on each seat.

Your program should include text about the bride and groom, the list of names of those involved in the processional (with the music accompanying them), the order of the ceremony events, the recessional music, and a thank-you note from the bride and groom. It's also nice to designate a section to tell a little about the venue. This is optional, but if you are in a particular unique space, the background story would be a great touch to include. People love knowing something about where they are!

Tutera Tip: Incorporate famous love quotes. I have done this before, and guests have collected the printed material and sent it back to the bride and groom in a scrapbook of printed materials with love quotes, along with pictures of the wedding and personal notes.

Listing the Wedding Party

The main reason for a program is to introduce, through literature, those involved in your wedding party whom all your guests will witness participating. The names of the bride and groom should appear on the cover of the program. On the inside, the names of your party should follow.

A STANDARD WEDDING PARTY TEMPLATE

Officiant
Reverend Thomas Tiller

Honored Grandparents
Charles and Sherry Corrigan
Grandparents of the Groom

Mark and Debbie Day
Grandparents of the Bride

Parents of the Groom
Christopher and Jennifer Corrigan

Maid of Honor
Laura Wedin

Best Man
James Corrigan

Bridesmaids and Groomsmen

Katie Schafer	Russell Davis
LeaAnn Ormaner	Randy Corrigan
Catherine McGee	Brian Torgersen
Julie Farley	Nick Carbaugh

Junior Bridesmaid

Melanie Dierks

Flower Girls

Amy Cheung and Kristen Mitchell

Ring Bearer

Michael Carisetti

Parents of the Bride

Matthew and Cate Jackson

Wedding Traditions

Explaining and detailing the traditions or meaningful elements of your ceremony not only involves your guests but also tells them more about you and your groom. Especially if some of your traditions are culturally symbolic and/or may not be familiar to all of your guests, describing what they will be witnessing helps them share in your ceremony and understand what they are seeing. Traditions like lighting a unity candle, standing under a chuppah, breaking a glass, taking Communion, jumping the broom, and exchanging rings are all interesting for your guests to learn more about.

To Our Dear Friends and Family . . .

The bride and the groom should always write a message to the guests joining them on their special day. This is one of the few moments when the guests get to "hear" the voice of the couple speaking directly to them. Use this time to share your gratitude for their efforts to be with you and for their love and friendship. The bride and groom may also take the opportunity to thank their parents in the program.

In Loving Memory . . .

Last, the bride and groom often acknowledge in their programs loved ones who have passed on. Something as simple as "In Loving Memory: We feel you surround us at all times, guiding and protecting us and showering us with your love. Today, we are particularly grateful that you touched our lives so deeply, both on earth and as our angels above" relays a memorial message that is still uplifting.

Sign and Date

At the end of your acknowledgments, include a signature from the bride and the groom: "With all our love, Kelly and John."

Unique Program Ideas

The program is an area of your wedding where you can express your creativity! Through your text, you have conveyed your voice as a couple, and now you can portray your style through presentation and display. Here are some top program display options:

- Create a traditional booklet with a coordinating ribbon and tassel.
- Use a scroll design.
- Print your text on a fan with a handle made of bamboo, birch, twig, or lucite. Have your handle be the coordination between your program and your ceremony style.

Tutera Tip: Write a different cherished love poem in calligraphy on individual paper fans. Just secure a twig "handle" between two sturdy sheets of paper that match the menus and place cards (the poem should be written on one in advance), then fasten

them together with rubber cement. Punch a hole on either side of
the twig and then tie a sheer white ribbon around it. Leave one
on each seat.

- Display programs in a beautiful open paper pouch that matches the design of the wedding. For an outdoor wedding, use a simple satin ribbon to tie one program to the inside of each guest's chair at the ceremony so it will stay secure and not blow away in the wind.
- Incorporate in the programs a continuous logo, monogram, or element (seashells, butterflies, leaves) that is used throughout your wedding.

Tutera Tip: This is where your hostess comes in. Choose someone special
who is not a bridesmaid to hand out programs (a perfect job for
a younger lady to execute).

PLACES, EVERYONE!:
ESCORT CARDS AND PLACE CARDS

For a more formal wedding, I love to have place cards for each guest. It takes time—lots of time—but is a very special touch for dinner receptions. Escort cards and place cards let the guests know that you took the time to think about the seating and socializing. It also creates a more comfortable environment, so guests don't have to search for a seat or wonder where they should sit.

Escort cards come first: They are placed in alphabetical order, on a table in front of the entrance of your reception. Guests choose their name card and discover their table number, which correlates with a numbered table inside the venue. The goal is to make the guests feel welcome, expected, and appreciated while also making it convenient for them to find where they should be without wandering aimlessly around. I know many brides like unique escort card ideas. I definitely suggest not doing charts and posted seating arrangements (and the corporate event feeling that goes along with them), but getting too creative can be confusing. Stay away from clumsy or disorganized escort cards (things like cards hanging from trees are clever but tough to follow) and keep it simple and tasteful.

Tutera Tip: *Guests should obtain their escort cards after the ceremony, so they don't lose or forget where to go prior to dinner.*

Your escort cards are a place to be a bit more traditional, not necessarily in design but in execution. There are two traditional ways to doing escort cards:

- A small card in an envelope. Shapes can vary. The guest name is on the outside of the envelope, and his or her table number is printed on the card inside.
- A panel card (no envelope). The card is either laid flat or propped up as a tent card. The guest's name is on the front and the table number is on the inside if tented.

Place cards are a wonderful detail, but require precision to execute! These name cards are set at each guest's place setting at the table to indicate where specifically the guest should sit.

Tutera Tip: *Use your logo on your escort cards and place cards to keep the momentum.*

WHAT'S COOKING?: MENU CARDS

Place cards can also be menu cards: a two-in-one printed item. By printing the guest name centered atop each menu card, it is as if you are inviting them to sit down and enjoy a meal just for them. This is a very elegant touch that is one of my personal favorites.

On each menu card, include the names of the bride and groom, the date of the wedding . . . and you could add a clever quote or saying, like "Eat, drink, and be married!" Say what each course is, followed by a description, and show all choices of the entrée (if there are choices). List the dessert course as "Followed by dessert" along with the name of the dessert, and if moving the dessert location, add "Please join us for dessert and dancing" and the respective new venue. If your wedding is formal, print the paired wine with each course on your menu card.

MS. SARA WIST

MENU

Adam and Alicia's Wedding
Friday, February 16, 2010
The ParkView Hotel
Charlotte, North Carolina

Appetizer
Summer Roll, Crispy Rock Shrimp, Nam Pla Sauce
Fresh summer roll of beets, cucumber, carrot, and basil;
salad of crispy fried rock shrimp tossed in miso chile dressing.
Served with nam pla dipping sauce.

Salad
Banana Frisée Salad
Crumbled feta, tender chunks of bananas, heart of palm, frisée,
cilantro leaves tossed in a grapefruit vinaigrette dressing

Entree
Braised Short Rib of Beef
Braised short rib of beef with crispy crab wontons
and a spicy tomato and coconut salad

Dessert
Wedding Cake

Crispy Pavlova with Key Lime Curd,
Blueberries, Basil, and Mint

Regardless of whether they are personalized or simply detailing the courses, each menu card sits on the charger plate at each guest's place setting. Don't print just one or two and place them in the middle of the table. It may feel like a diner! Each guest should always get his or her own. Display them in a pocket fold of the napkin atop each plate. To enhance each guest's dining space, menu cards should be created with the following general dimensions and shapes:

VERTICAL MENU CARD
A traditional choice.
Suggested size: 9×5 inches.

HORIZONTAL MENU CARD

A modern choice.

Suggested size: 4×8 inches.

SQUARE MENU CARD

A contemporary choice.

Suggested size: 6×6 inches.

THE PAPER TRAIL: ACCENTS AND MORE

Personalized cocktail napkins and restroom hand towels are a great extra detail to offer.

Tutera Tip: For a more personal touch, add a favorite quote (from a famous person, or one of your own) to one or more of the various custom paper goods: invitations, menu cards, cocktail napkins, place cards, gift bags, and so on. It will add a little something for your guests to talk about. You can find famous thematic quotes online or in books of quotations.

MUCH OBLIGED: THANK-YOU NOTES

When ordering invitations for a party at which you will receive gifts, remember to order thank-you notes that match the design. It's a terrific final touch and usually results in savings when ordered at the same time. Guests will receive your matching cards and remember your wedding design and the experience they had with you on your day.

Writing hundreds of thank-you notes (or even writing twenty thank-you notes) can be a process, so help yourself ahead of time as much as you can. Look back to that original guest list and address list of people you invited, and use a copy of those lists as you open your gifts to keep track of who gave you what. Better yet, to truly enjoy the moment, enlist a family member to jot down who gave what as you and your husband open and enjoy each gift without worrying about recording all the details. Whoever is taking notes, be sure they are specific. Use colors, brand names, and descriptive words so when you go back to the mountainous heap of gratitude you owe, each note is already half written with the description of your gifts. Your note recipients will be glad to know that the gift they selected for you didn't get lost in the shuffle, that you noticed exactly what it was, and that you truly are grateful.

Tutera Tip: Handwrite every thank-you note. Your guests will appreciate the effort! They put effort into picking out a gift for you, and will notice the effort they get back!

To this day, my mother says, "You can't use it, spend it, or play with it unless you have sent a note thanking the person for it!" While some of your gifts may take time to use because they may not be needed until a special occasion, thank-you notes should still be sent no later than one year after your wedding. Six months is the time frame to keep in good etiquette, though the sooner the better! If you get any gifts before your wedding, it is perfectly acceptable (and helpful to you later) if you write the thank-you note right away, even if the guest will receive it before the wedding. But take "note": If you have special monogrammed cardstock with your new married initials on it, it is considered poor form to use it before you are officially united, so keep it for postwedding notes.

Your notes don't have to be lengthy written conversations of obligation—just simple, three-line notes of gratitude that mention (a) how glad you are that the guest was able to attend your wedding (or how much you missed him or her), (b) how much you appreciate the specific gift, and (c) how thankful you are that they contributed to your happily ever after and your happiness together overall. If you receive money, the general rule of thumb is to always mention how you may use it, or how you did use it and how much you enjoyed using it/how much it benefited you. You do not need to note the denomination of how much they gave you.

Tutera Tip: *Always make sure your thank-you notes are signed by the both of you! Even if they're written by one person, sign both your names.*

Tutera Tip: *Do not send thank-you notes before you are married, as you are not officially husband and wife. You can prepare them ahead of time and mail them out after your wedding.*

Then signed, sealed, delivered: It's yours!

Six

FASHION FORWARD

THE AISLE IS YOUR RUNWAY

Ta-da! Your walk down the aisle is your grand entrance as a bride and a soon-to-be Mrs.

It's your much anticipated and buzzed-about arrival. Your friends and loved ones are all gathered to see you, and everyone waits for the singular moment when the doors open and the music swells. All eyes are on you as you appear looking like a heavenly vision of bridal beauty . . . This is your big scene! The cameras will flash, the guests will rise (a guarantee!), and you'll head straight down the aisle—ready to strut your stuff down your own personal catwalk, filled with confidence, excitement, and joy. Just like everyone on the red carpet asks "What are you wearing?!," your version is very similar—everyone will notice what you step out in and how you carry yourself—so for your big debut, get ready to choose your gown and be fashionably fabulous every step of the way!

MAKING YOUR DEBUT:
YOUR BRIDAL GOWN!

They say the moment you try on "the" dress—you just know. It's a magical feeling that can elicit tears or cheers of joy (depending on how long it took you to find the thing!). This is about more than just looking good—it's about the gown that makes you feel the most beautiful you have ever felt, about the one special time you get to be the center of attention beyond compare, and about the moment when your husband-to-be lays his eyes on you for the first time as his bride . . . you will want to be looking gorgeous for that moment of your life that will live on forever.

There are a lot more "I Do's" than "I Don'ts" when finding your wedding gown. After you read the one hard-and-fast "I Don't" that I can't let you forget, enjoy discovering all the wonderful things you *should* do when picking the perfect gown for your perfect day!

I DON'Ts for purchasing Your Wedding Gown
- Don't bring everyone you've ever known dress shopping with you. Though it is an exciting moment, you'll get lots of feedback (and end up more confused about choosing what you want!). Bring a few trusted advisers—your mom, your aunt, your sister—and keep it small (things can get over-whelming when you bring a whole entourage into a small wedding boutique—or even a large one, for that matter!). If you want to include lots of people in the process, go once with a minimal group of people, narrow down your selec-tions, and have others join you as you make the final choices (or bring them with you to the fitting or the veil shopping after all is said and done with the gown!). It's important to

stay true to the bride inside and not fall in love with a dress just because everyone says you look great in it (oh, what a problem to have!). It has to be the dress that makes *you* feel like a million dollars inside and out, no matter what the audience says!

I DO's for Purchasing Your Wedding Gown

- Take note of the dress-ordering timeline. Many brides forget that dresses take six to eight months to order and then they need to be fitted, altered, and bustled by a seamstress. Begin early (but not so early that you second-guess your choice or your tastes change by the time your wedding comes) to avoid rushing—it can get very costly in stress and fees!
- Consider having two dresses: your ceremony gown, and a party dress. More and more brides are having fun with the "wedding dress concept" and wearing a traditional full gown for the ceremony, and then changing into something fun, sassier, and more comfortable (and appropriate for dancing all night in) at the reception. This means a whole new look: new dress, new shoes, new jewelry, even a change in hairstyle (and I have a feeling that most ladies won't say no to more fun with fashion). Stay with the white color so you are still in the bridal spotlight when you put on your party dress and your dancing shoes!
- Familiarize yourself with the general terms of dresses before you go so that you can either help the bridal consultant find what you want, or so you can go in sounding like an educated bride (who won't get ripped off!).

YOUR DEFINING MOMENT: A DRESS CUT GLOSSARY

Empire Waist. A high waistline lies just below the bust, and then the rest of the dress falls straight down to the hem. Empire waists are best on girls who are slender on top or petite because this style creates the illusion of length. It also is good to hide a bottom-heavy figure or a thicker waist.

A-line. A slight flare in the skirt starts from a narrow waist or from the shoulders. Streamlined and flattering, A-lines are ideal for highlighting a narrow waist and skimming over thighs.

Basque Waist. This dropped waist starts right at or right below your natural waistline, and dips in the center creating a V or a rounded U shape. The basque waist can look like a corset or a bodice, and is ideal for the princess look.

Sheath. A sheath is form fitting to the natural curves of your body, but does not have a determinant shape like the defined A-line or empire waist. It's more free-flowing and often used with lighter, sheer fabrics.

YOUR DEFINING MOMENT: A FABRIC GLOSSARY

Silk. A light, flowing, luxurious matte fabric that is used for an airy look. Silk is ideal for draping and soft looks.

Chiffon. A graceful fabric of sheer silk or rayon.

Organza. A sheer, stiff fabric of silk or synthetic material. Organza is strong yet has a delicate appearance and the ability to give off sheen.

Taffeta. A crisp, lustrous fabric. Taffeta comes in a variety of colors, and is a bold statement fabric.

Satin. A fabric typically with a glossy surface and a dull back. Satin is softer than taffeta, but more opaque, bold, and strong. Most wedding gowns are made of satin, which is durable and elegant.

Duchess Satin. A heavy, lustrous, rich-looking satin weave.

YOUR DEFINING MOMENT: A BUSTLE GLOSSARY

Bustles are worn under the skirt of a dress in the back, just below the waist, to keep the skirt from dragging. Originally popular in the mid- to late 1800s when women wore full dresses and gowns, bustles are used for weddings now postceremony to keep the train of the gown from getting dirty or in the way of walking and dancing.

Traditional Bustle. The traditional bustle is a gathering of your train that is attached to the back of your gown. Imagine pinching a part of your train, and attaching the pinched fabric to the back of your dress (around the waist) to create a pretty cascade of fabric that also frees up your movements for dancing. Your seamstress can demonstrate for you what a traditional bustle would look like on your dress: For some detailed trains, a bustle highlights the embellishment by bringing it to floor length. Traditional bustles can be secured to the outside back of your dress with discreet buttons, ties, snaps, or hook-and-eye attachments.

French or Inverted Bustle. Often called an underbustle, the French bustle hooks up under the skirt (as opposed to over the skirt, as the traditional bustle does). For this type of bustle, gathers of fabric are brought to the inside of the dress, and the extra material is tacked underneath your skirt and secured with a series of strategically spaced ties, buttons, snaps, or hooks. The attachments are inside near the center-back seam. A French bustle often looks "fluffier" than the traditional bustle. The French bustle should be used for long trains with large skirts or short trains on sleek dresses. If your gown does not have a waist seam to attach the bustle to, a French (inverted) bustle will do the job. It's also ideal for gowns with train decoration right below the waist area; where traditional bustles would cover the embellishments, the inverted would highlight them.

Detachable and Removable Trains. Some trains are completely removable, leaving behind a fully intact skirt. These trains are usually snapped or tacked on around the waistline, or the removable length is attached by a hidden layering in part of the skirt design.

The biggest downfall to bride's fashion is mismatching dress and body type. Know your body shape and what styles work best on you before you go dress shopping. The key is to flatter your body and work with what you've got to look amazing in a fashion piece that complements your every move. There are four main body shapes: apple, pear, ruler, and hourglass. Which one are you, and which dress styles will you look best in?

Tutera Tip: Show your support! Ask your bridal consultant to provide you with the right undergarments. This is very important and can prevent a fashion faux pas! No Janet Jackson Super Bowl replays, please!

Tutera Tip: For the long "button down the back" look without the hassle of fastening every single button, look for gowns with hidden zippers, or ask for one to be sewn in so you can have that beautiful look with ease on your wedding day.

Do I Have To Wear White? Matching Dress Hue to Your Complexion

Did you know there are over two hundred shades of white in bridal gowns? It's true. With so many options, may no bride ever say, "I don't look good in white"! The traditional white gown dates back to the eighteenth century, when white was a symbol of status and wealth. Having the ability to wear and risk getting a white dress dirty was a sign that the family could afford to have such garments. Through the centuries, brides of various countries and cultures have worn blue, red, and even green, though the traditional American

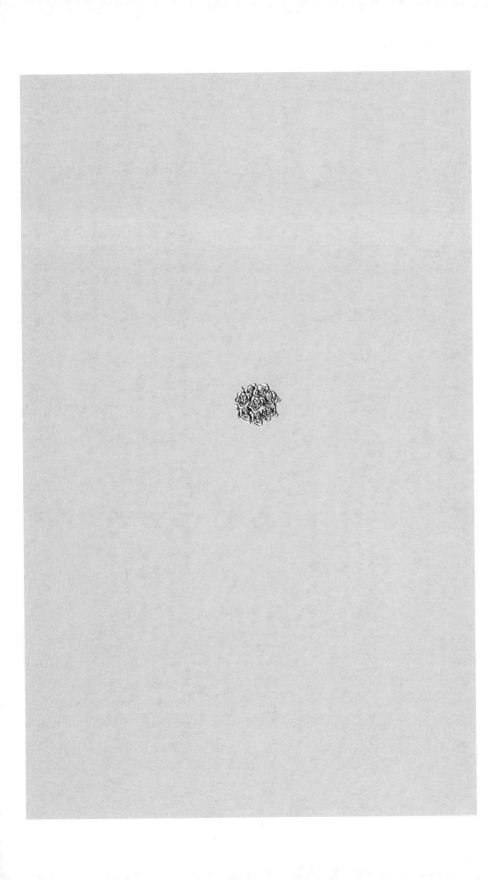

Body Type	Characteristics	I DO's	I DON'Ts	Overall Tips	Celebrities Shaped Like This
Apple	Full face and neck Broad shoulders Full chest Undefined waist with narrower hips Flat backside Shapely legs Upper body with a larger frame than lower body	Tops with detail or movement, either in fabric or embellishment Fitted corsets and bodices (as long as they are not too tight) Drop and V-necklines that pull attention away from your shoulders and down your torso Empire or raised waists (the grown-up version of the "babydoll" look) that bring the eye up	You radiate in simple style! Avoid gowns that play up the puffiness and fullness that unnecessarily make your upper body appear bigger than it is. Avoid large ballroom skirts and tulle; stick to A-lines and great empire waists. Don't wear veils that end at the widest part of your hips, which would accentuate them visually.	Look for gowns with detailing around the waist. A cinched waist or a tie around the waist gives a slimming look. Veils that fall right below your waist or even to midthigh are perfect for you!	Catherine Zeta-Jones Drew Barrymore Elizabeth Hurley Tyra Banks
Pear	Long or slender neck Sloping or narrow shoulders Narrow back Small to medium bust Defined waist	Gowns with necklines that are scooped, draped, V-necked, rounded, or squared. (Any lower or wider neckline will look great as it will emphasize your upper body and draw attention to your face.) Halter tops	Stay away from body-hugging gowns (the mermaid) that will only show every bump and curve. Also steer away from full skirts (ballgowns).	A-line and flared gowns look best on pears. When choosing a dress, try on empire waists or wrap dresses that flow over the hip area. Say yes to embellishments and detailing! Gowns with a lot going on above the waist, in embroidery, beading, or fabric texture will balance your lower half.	Kristin Davis Shakira Jennifer Lopez Beyoncé

Body Type	Characteristics	What to Wear	What to Avoid	Tips	Celebrities
	Curvy hips and backside Full legs Lower body with a larger frame than upper body	Wide-set straps Loose-fitting fabrics (sheers and organza) Fitted dress tops		Always choose sleek shoes. A fabulous pair of strappy sandals with a thin heel will work for you better visually than a chunky heel or clunky toe.	Kate Moss Gwyneth Paltrow Courteney Cox Cameron Diaz Julia Roberts Keira Knightley Hilary Swank
Ruler	Full neck Broad back Regular bust Undefined waist Overall balanced figure Great legs and arms	Dropped or cinched waists Spaghetti straps A-line gowns with a bit of a flare, gathered at the waist Tops that give the illusion of curves V-necks that emphasize bust and draw attention to your face Gowns that draw focus to your great legs and thighs	Avoid the extremes! Nix gowns that are too clingy or tight on top, and steer clear of loose gowns (sheaths and empire waists) that do not show off your curves. Choose dresses with shape to give you shape!	Gowns with tops that are fitted at the waist (like the mermaid cut) give the appearance of a curvier figure. Look for bodices that give shape to your torso, with boning or preexisting shape. Sashes, bows, and trim around your waist also create shapely hips.	

(continued)

Body Type	Characteristics	I DO's	I DON'Ts	Overall Tips	Celebrities Shaped Like This
Hour-glass	Symmetrical shoulders and hips Full, shapely bust Distinctly defined waist Medium to broad hips Hips proportionate to shoulders Shapely legs	Gowns that enhance your bust and waist Tops with V-necks or scooped necklines Halter tops will look great and show off your shoulders Butterfly cuts (gowns with a long design or creases in the front) that add height	Stay away from gowns that are too loose or overwhelming in size—they will only make you look frumpy and hide your beautiful curves. Pass on short veils that will shorten your look, and avoid ruffles and bustline details. With embellishments, select small dots, crystals, or patterns for a soft and slimming look.	Many dress styles work with your body type; just remember your goal! Accentuate your body and the curves you already have. Look for gowns with bodices that sit at your waist or lengthen your body (like drop waists and basque waists).	Jessica Simpson Salma Hayek Scarlett Johansson

bride has since been seen in white, which symbolizes happiness, joy, and purity.

Now brides wear other colors, such as soft blush pink, champagne gold, antique white, lavender, or even white adorned with colorful threading and appliqué as a fashion statement and testament to their individual personalities and preferences. Wear whichever color you choose, as long as it reflects who you are, inside and out.

When choosing shades of white, remember that just because you are a bride doesn't mean you have to have a stark white dress. Pure white goes with some skin tones, while natural white or ivory is best with others. Don't be afraid of choosing an off-white gown. At the wedding, you will be the only one wearing any shade of white, and it will register as traditional white to the guests. Find out which shade complements you best so you can order the appropriate color. Ask your dress shop for swatches so you can get an idea of each designer's tones. Take them home with you to hold next to your skin in various lights.

Which Shade of White Matches Your Skin Tone?

Skin Tone	Dress Color
Fair	Ivory, Off-White, Antique White
Medium	White, Antique White, Antique Gold, Off-White, Ivory
Dark	White, Antique White, Antique Gold, Blush Pink
Olive	White, Ivory, Off-White

Over Hill and Veil: Finding Your Veil

During the times of arranged marriages, the bride's face was covered until the groom was committed to her at the ceremony (some people say it was to prevent the groom from running away from an ugly bride, but we really know there are no ugly brides and certainly you are not one!). The tradition that it is "bad luck" for the groom to see the bride before the wedding day still stands and thus, the veil is used as concealment. The other story behind the veil is that it was intended to protect the bride from evil spirits. People were so closely tied to this superstition (I suppose we are still to this day . . . no bride ever wants a thing to go wrong with their wedding day) that bridesmaids were introduced as "decoys" to fool any lurking evildoers. These maids would not wear veils but would be dressed attractively and would be prepared to sacrifice their souls if required (and boy, do we know there's some truth to that when your maid of honor has given up her fourth weekend in a row to give you advice on which white shoe you should buy).

Blushing brides: The blusher (the piece of the veil that traditionally covers the bride's face) was once thought to protect the bride on her way to the ceremony. Now, the blusher is more of a fashion statement, entirely optional for the bride to wear. Veils can be created with or without a blusher—and some brides would rather have no veil at all!

Tutera Tip: During the ceremony, the groom traditionally lifts the bride's blusher right after the "you may kiss the bride" announcement. As the blusher also signifies the bride's youth, innocence, and/or submission to the husband, a bride lifting her own veil can translate to their equality and her independence.

Tutera Tip: When donning various dresses and veils at the store, look at yourself in the mirror from all angles, not just the front. Remember that you will be standing facing the officiant, with your back to the "audience" the entire time, and the detailing of the back of your dress, your train, and the appearance of your veil is what everyone will be seeing the most of during your entire ceremony. If showing the back of your gown is important to you, choose a sheer veil that allows the details of your dress to show through.

YOUR DEFINING MOMENT: A VEIL GLOSSARY

Cathedral. The most formal, longest veil. This veil falls down toward your train, below floor length and beyond. . . .

Chapel. A long, formal veil that extends to floor length.

Waltz. This veil falls between the bride's knee and the ankle. One length shorter than the chapel veil.

Fingertip. A very popular length that extends past the waist to the fingertips. This veil is both formal and manageable.

Elbow-Length. A veil that falls to the bride's elbow, typically about 25 to 28 inches long.

Flyaway. A shoulder-length, multilayered veil. The flyaway veil is not as formal as the other longer styles.

Waterfall, Cascade, or Fountain. Not a length, but the style of gathering of veil fabric that creates a cascade of fabric on either side of the face. Shoulder or elbow-length is the appropriate length for this veil effect.

Tutera Tip: Keep fire safety in mind when wearing a veil—candles and veils in close proximity can be a recipe for disaster! Be aware of your surroundings in your veil, tack down candles, and use hurricane glasses for the candles that will be close to you at the altar and reception.

AMOROUS ADDITIONS: ACCESSORIES

Accessories can bring out your personality and your overall wedding style through a variety of "additions"! In both concrete ways like fashion pieces (or lack thereof) and in the subtle detailing of jewelry and little special touches, accessories are accents of you.

Wraps and shawls are fashionable options for the conservative wedding. These quick cover-ups can also be items that bridesmaids use time and again. When in doubt, cover up to avoid awkward exposure; some churches require conservative dress and some guests (particularly older audiences and guests at second marriages) may be more comfortable in a less modern, less revealing setting.

Tutera Tip: Straps can be attached to a strapless gown by buttons on the inside, making an easy switch from a strapless ceremony gown to a functional and supportive strappy one for the reception (for lots of dancing!).

Pass It On: Heirloom Pieces

Incorporating special artifacts from your ancestors adds deep sentiment to your accessories and further makes your wedding day exclusively yours. Many times, veils, jewelry, beads, and trinkets can be used as is, but if you have an heirloom piece that is no longer in style (yet is still close to your heart!), just get creative. Your grandmother's rosary beads or brooch can stay intact while wrapped around the handle of your bridal bouquet. An older veil can be adapted into a new veil, or restored by a professional. (Of course, first make sure that altering the heirloom is something that is okay to do; especially if there is no going back, you want to be absolutely certain!)

Play to the old adage "Something old, something new, something borrowed, something blue"! Have fun finding elements to fit each saying. For example:

Something Old. Heirloom pieces are perfect for "something old": a jewelry piece, a swatch of fabric from your mom's wedding dress wrapped around your bouquet handle, a penny in your shoe.

Something New. Your new gown, your veil, a photo in a locket of you and your groom, a pair of fabulous new shoes.

Something Borrowed. Your mother's wedding band on your right hand, a piece of jewelry, a tiara, a purse from a bridesmaid.

Something Blue. A bit of blue in your jewelry or hairpiece, a blue flower used in your bouquet, light blue embellishments on your garter, a pretty handkerchief with blue stitching.

Diamonds Are a Girl's Best Friend: Jewelry

Jewelry can create a statement yet also be a very personal way to send a subtle message or make a special tribute to someone or something. Perhaps you will wear the same strand of pearls your mother wore on her wedding day, or you might adorn yourself with the first bracelet your fiancé ever gave you in your relationship. Jewelry can be a special, emotional, and beautiful element to your ceremony and wedding day.

If you prefer to head straight to the store to get something sparkly and new (which isn't a bad thing, either!), choose what makes you happy and you'll create new memories with your wedding jewels. This is the day to look like royalty! Wear chandelier earrings or a gorgeous drop pendant, but be wary as you select dynamic pieces: Some dresses don't even need necklaces, and some great earrings will be enough glitz to last you. Go ahead and get glamorous, but don't overdo the jewelry and make *too* many statements.

If the Shoe Fits, Wear It!

Choose your bridal shoes carefully for color, comfort, and style! Bridal shoes can be as ornate as your dress, or as practical as your undergarments. Your shoe mission, should you choose to accept it, is to find the perfect pair that is both. Bridal shoes come in several shades of white to match the various tones of wedding dresses. Take a swatch of your dress with you as you choose your shoes, and test them out as a whole so you don't discover the day of that they aren't the right shade. If you're having trouble finding a good match, it may be easier to have your local dress or shoe shop dye white shoes to match exactly.

I DO's for Shoes

- Weeks before the wedding, wear your bridal shoes to break them in to avoid aching feet and prevent blisters from first-time wear occuring on your big day.
- Purchase your shoes (and your undergarments, slips, and other accoutrements, for that matter) before your first fitting with your gown seamstress—you want to make sure your hem is done to the right length that matches the shoe height you will wear on your wedding day.
- Some bridesmaid gown designers also sell matching purses or clutches: perfect gifts for bridesmaids.
- If you choose to have shoes or purses dyed to match your bridesmaid gowns, after the wedding, tell them to dye them black so they can use them again.

I DON'Ts for Shoes

- Please, pretty please, don't switch to sneakers or flip-flops when it's reception time. Maintain your prettiness and poise, and don't change into backyard barbeque bride.
- Don't be taller than your groom if you can avoid it! Make sure your heel height is appropriate for standing next to your groom. Grab the pair you'll wear right now and test it out!

FASHION FOR YOUR BRIDAL PARTY

Now, I know you would *never ever* be like the one bride who once told me she purposefully wanted her bridal party to look worse than she did so she would look the best! Shame on her, and thank goodness that's not you! Remember, through this whole process you want your girls to *love* you and to love that they said yes to being in your party (and to love the role they play within it!). This is where the "bridezilla" often comes out of misguided bridal belles. Make sure you end up with stronger friendships—not weaker ones.

When selecting bridesmaid dresses for a bunch of different women, it's likely that you now have all those body types together and have to try to fit them into one dress style. At the end of the day, you want your girls to look great! Work on finding a dress that works for them all, or choose different styles that are in the same fabric and color. This is your supporting cast, and you need them to look and feel amazing. It will help them give you the support you need on your day.

Pick out dresses with style and taste. Poor Jane, Katherine Heigl's loyal-to-a-fault character in the movie *27 Dresses*, with a closet full of hideous bridesmaid gowns so tacky, one must wonder if there was some truth to her boyfriend asking her if one of the themes of the wedding was "humiliation." I have a dear friend who just discovered she could use one of her old bridesmaid dresses cut up and repurposed as a great Christmas tree skirt. While it may not be true that bridesmaid gowns are "easy to wear again," using them as a holiday decoration is probably not the ultimate destination you want for your girls' gowns (and for their money spent on participating in your wedding). Honestly, your taste may differ from the next girl, but the blunt point is that some things are universally ugly. While you can't please everyone all the time, you can please more than just yourself—be appealing to the eye as well!

DRESS TIPS FOR SMILING BRIDES AND BRIDESMAIDS
- Choose different styles of dresses in the same colors
- Select varying colors that complement each girl, but keep a consistent style
- Have gown colors be different but all within the same shade
- Choose dresses composed of "separates" and allow girls to order skirts in one size and tops in another
- Alternate sash styles and colors

- Encourage your bridesmaids to choose their bust style, if available

YOUR DEFINING MOMENT: A BRIDESMAID DRESS NECKLINE GLOSSARY

Sweetheart. A neckline that resembles the top of a heart along the bust line.

Halter. A neckline in which two straps or pieces of the dress (from spaghetti straps to ribbons) meet and are secured together behind the neck. This is the most flattering style for the most people.

Strapless. A neckline with no straps; exposes shoulders.

Off-the-Shoulder. Open neckline, with fabric resting on (not covering) shoulders.

I DO's for Bridesmaid Dresses

- Give your bridesmaids enough time in advance to order their gowns (and also stash some cash to purchase them!). Bridesmaid dresses usually take three to four months to get in, and then each dress needs to be fitted and altered.
- Pay attention to bridesmaid-dress dye lots. Ask to order all the bridesmaid dresses together to avoid the risk of getting various shades of your dress color.
- Order swatches of your bridesmaid dresses before ordering the bridesmaid flowers—take the swatches to the florist when choosing which flowers will complement the dress best.
- Find a way to thank your ladies for participating in your wedding and for spending the money (on the dress and accessories) to make your day just the way you want it.
- Save extra fabric scraps from alterations to wrap your bridesmaids flower bouquet handles and make them a perfect match.

I DON'Ts for Bridesmaid Dresses

* Don't think that bustles are just for brides! They are, in fact, for bridesmaids, too. If their dresses are long and formal with a bit of a train, don't forget their comfort and safety in dancing at the reception and encourage them to get their trains buttoned up as well.

Junior Bridesmaids

Junior bridesmaids are typically aged nine to thirteen: too old to be a flower girl and too young to be a bridesmaid. Dress your junior bridesmaid in a modernized or youthful version of the bridesmaid dresses, or in a monochromatic but different shade of the bridesmaid dress color. For example, pink would be a more youthful junior bridesmaid dress shade to match burgundy bridesmaid dresses. Steer clear from dressing the young ladies in anything too revealing. As opposed to carbon copies of mature adults, they are classy young ladies coming up into society.

Flower Girls and Ring Bearers

Flower girl and ring bearer fashions are sweet and simple, just like the children in the roles. Little kids are adorable scene stealers no matter what they wear, but especially so in formal wear. Pick out a sweet and simple dress for your flower girl, and as for the little man: Take him to a tux shop to get his measurements and his own fitting (he may enjoy going with the "guys" or may need a separate visit to avoid being overwhelmed). Don't forget to have them both practice with the flower girl basket of petals and the ring bearer pillow for their big debuts.

READY FOR MY CLOSE-UP:
HAIR AND MAKEUP

In the 1950s black-and-white movie *Sunset Boulevard* Gloria Swanson uttered famous words during her portrayal of starlet Norma Desmond.

As she proclaims that her life is for the stage and screen, she exclaims, "You see, this is my life! It always will be! Nothing else! Just us, the cameras, and those wonderful people out there in the dark! All right, Mr. DeMille, I'm ready for my close-up."

Oh, how wonderful it would be if every day of our lives we could all dramatically build up to a line that calls makeup artists, hair stylists, and rolling cameras to project our beauty to a million adoring fans! Your wedding day is your moment to capture all that glamour, prestige, and pampering. Like Norma Desmond's devoted public, your guests, groom, photographers, and videographers will be making you the star of the night, so call upon your dream team of beauticians to make you look and feel your best. It's time for you to get ready for *your* close-up!

I DO's for Hair

- Have a trial! Take time to have your hair done exactly as your hairdresser will do it on the day of your wedding so you know precisely what you are getting (and how long it will take). No surprises on your wedding day when it comes to how you look—the only one surprised should be your groom!
- When having an afternoon wedding, arrange ahead of time for your hair and makeup stylist to be available for you early— most salons do not open until 9 or 10 A.M., which might not allow you enough time to relax, fully prepare yourself and your bridesmaids, and get to the ceremony on time.
- When scheduling your hair appointments for your actual day, add a cushion of time so no one (you or your bridesmaids) will be "fashionably late."
- For your wedding day, wear a button-down shirt or dress when you get your hair done—that way, when you change into your wedding dress, there is no pulling of shirts over your finished hairdo.
- If you are wearing a tiara, have the hairdresser style your hair around your tiara first, then attach the veil separately,

so that postceremony you can remove the veil and still make use of the beautiful tiara in your hair.

I DON'Ts for Hair

- Don't assume anything when it comes to wedding day hairstyles. Collect photos of celebrity hairstyles you like. Bringing in images will help your stylist identify what you want. Terms like "big bun," "soft waves," "sophisticated," and "chic" mean different things to different people, so comparing pictures is the best way to communicate.
- Speak up! Explain the style of your wedding, your gown, and your reception to your hairdresser. Ask him or her to suggest hairdos that will match your wedding overall.

I DO'S for Makeup

- Some stylists may not want to leave a salon on your wedding day. Ask your wedding coordinator or friends if they know of someone who makes house (or venue) calls.
- Schedule a consultation and try to book that consultation on a day when you have a fitting or shower. There are usually fees for consultations, so plan for yours to happen when you have something special going on, or when you can test it out with your dress. Get your money's worth!
- When you go for a trial, wear a white tank top without a collar. The white color reflects the color of your wedding dress and makes a big difference as you picture how you will look in your gown. (Your reflection also may look odd to you when you see yourself wearing street clothes with full bridal makeup, which may skew your judgment when deciding to go heavier or lighter.)
- Bring a camera on your trial day, and take photos from all angles.
- Do have your nails done to match the style of your makeup, dress, and wedding. Try out your manicure before your

wedding day. Paint your nails the color you think you want, and hold them next to your dress before your actual wedding day to make sure it's what goes best.

- Create an order of who in your bridal party will be made up first. Do mothers of the bride and groom first, and the flower girl toward the end (kids love to play with their hair and face, so the shorter amount of time between your flower girl's styling and the wedding, the better). You, as the bride, should be last.
- Start early on your wedding day and schedule enough time for your services to be done well. No one should be rushed, fearing that the clock is ticking. Allow yourself the right amount of time to be pampered properly.

I DON'Ts for Makeup

- Don't wait until the last minute! Book hair and makeup artists early. The good ones go fast!
- Don't skimp here—hire the right amount of makeup artists for your wedding party; having a rushed makeup job done on anyone (especially—gasp!—the bride) never ends well. Remember, all your bridesmaids will be in your wedding photos for life, and they, too, need to look picture perfect! Ask your makeup consultant in advance how much time he or she needs per girl, and how many assistants are needed to hire to get the job properly done with time to spare for touch-ups.
- Don't pick a hairstyle that's too high-maintenance for you— keep it simple for staying power. From ceremony to cake-cutting is a long day, so keep your hair and makeup simple to last.
- Don't overdo it. There is a reason the word "understated" was invented! Less is more, especially when it comes to your wedding makeup. You still need to look like *you*. You don't want to appear in your photos (and to all your guests) as

though someone else is playing the role of you. Stay true to your beautiful self.

- Don't forget to ask your makeup artist to use waterproof mascara to prevent streaks from those tears of joy!
- Don't be without what you need. Have a bridal emergency kit for your maid of honor to have in case anything goes awry! Items in your kit:
  - Extra pairs of hose
  - Clear nail polish and matching nail polish to manicures and pedicures
  - Erasers or extra earring backs
  - Wite-Out
  - Nail-polish remover
  - Makeup remover
  - Tissues and Q-tips
  - Scissors
  - Scotch tape
  - Needle and thread in various colors
  - Feminine hygiene items
  - Nail file
  - Hair spray
  - Face powder

MEN OF THE HOUR: GROOM AND GROOMSMEN

Well, it's highly unlikely you will ever have to hear a group of unruly gentlemen fighting over what style shoe to wear or debating if they should go with the wrap or bare-shouldered. Lucky for your groom (and for you!), the task of getting your gentlemen dressed to the nines is all his! How involved you become is up to you. I say leave them to their own devices, but lend them a discerning eye when it comes to matching colors and choosing styles if they need help.

YOUR DEFINING MOMENT: A MENSWEAR GLOSSARY

Suit. A jacket with trousers, usually matching. Includes tie.

Black Tie. Standard tuxedo wear: black tuxedo jacket, black slacks, white shirt. "Black Tie" is completed with black or matching vest and tie. This dress code means evening wear for both men and women.

White Tie. The most formal evening wear. It generally consists of a black dress coat, white shirt, white bow tie, and black slacks. (It is rarely suggested these days, but can be a very elegant look for weddings!)

Morning Suit. The daytime version of formal dress, worn to morning or afternoon social events before five o'clock. Formal day wear consists of a (usually) gray jacket, matching slacks, white shirt, and a tie.

I DO's for Tuxedos

- Have your groom wear an elegant vest and matching tie or bow tie.
- Choose a color variation for your groom's vest and your best man's vest to differentiate them slightly from the rest of your groomsmen. Many patterns can be done in various shades of the same color, and give a sense of unity but also uniqueness to the two leading men. Choose a color for your groomsmen's vests that matches the bridesmaid dresses. Take the bridesmaid dress (or a swatch of the fabric) into the tuxedo shop to choose the right hue.
- Choose sophisticated, proper suits—no *Saturday Night Fever* craziness! Go for timeless. (No bold patterns, no light blue or rust-red suits, and nothing made of velvet, no matter how "cool" the guys think he looks in it.)
- Make sure your gentlemen have the right accessories:

- Belt
- Cuff links
- Studs
- Tie or bow tie
- Vest
- Black shoes
- Black socks

I DON'Ts for Tuxedos

- Don't keep the plastic cuff links and studs from the rental store. You may consider allowing your groomsmen to use their own cuff links to add part of their personality to their attire, or even give cuff links, perhaps with a colored stone that coordinates with your wedding colors, as a nice groomsmen gift before the wedding.
- Don't wear a cummerbund—even though they are traditional, they tend to look messy, plus, they may translate to "high school prom" instead of "highly sophisticated wedding party"!

"EVERLASTING" LOVE: WEDDING GOWN PRESERVATION

Any woman who has ever owned anything white knows that after time, the white wardrobe turns to an off-white wardrobe or a dingy yellow wardrobe. Yuck! The thought of that happening to your incredible wedding gown is too much to bear, especially if someday you would like to have your daughter or granddaughter have the option of rewearing your gown or reworking it into a gown of her own.

Take your gown to a professional who does dress cleaning and preservation—get an evaluation and a quote, ask for references, and meet with their specialists before you relinquish your treasured gown. They will first clean your gown, treat stains, repair tears, and then put it on a bodice form to keep the shape before placing it in a special box (free from acid, sulfur, and other toxins that contribute to aging the fabric and discoloration). If you choose to store it yourself, make sure your box repels moisture, humidity, and moths.

There is less of a rush to bring in your gown for preservation than your bouquet, but the sooner the better, especially if there are stains (or stains you may not see) that need to be tended to. Years after your wedding, if you didn't get your gown preserved and you change your mind, you can bring it in for restoration (as opposed to preservation), but I always say—planning now is better for later!

If you are not partial to your gown enough to preserve it (or even keep it) I do suggest selling it or donating it to a special shop that resells preworn wedding dresses. Making Memories Breast Cancer Foundation—Brides Against Breast Cancer Nationwide Tour of Gowns (www.makingmemories.org) resells thousands of donated wedding gowns, with all proceeds from the wedding gown purchases going toward making wishes come true for breast cancer patients. Gently used wedding gowns can also be donated to a church, Goodwill, or the Salvation Army. Your gown will be resold at an affordable price to someone in need, and all profits support these organizations' ongoing work. Additionally, all donations are tax deductible. All these wonderful charities that provide preworn dresses for good causes would love your bridal and bridesmaid dresses (much more so than your Christmas tree would). Think of all the good marriage karma that will bring you!

Seven

STRIKE UP THE BAND: ENTERTAINMENT!

While we know that your wedding is all about showing the world the love and commitment you and your hubby-to-be have for each other (and also, of course, how good you look in white), it's also important to know that as host and hostess you have a "responsibility" to throw a great party to celebrate that love and show your guests a good time!

When it comes to entertainment, I always tell my brides that this is the part (besides getting to see you wed) where wedding guests decide they are glad they Rsvp'ed "yes" to an invitation. From serious ceremony to fabulous reception, the driving force is always the entertainment. Entertainment determines the "how" of your guests' involvement and the "what" of what makes the celebration engaging for them. We know they are there for you to support you on the biggest milestone of your life, but by all means, they should have a blast doing so as well! That is where you come in with making your evening a night to remember. Captivate them through music, dance, emotion, points of interest, culture, and—most important—through the wedding story you tell.

CEREMONY SERENADES

Music is the heartbeat to your wedding, creating the pace of your ceremony, keeping your party alive, and setting an audible "pulse" that correlates with the event flow. You can build or slow the energy of your wedding through music. As you choose your musical entertainment, you are doing the same as composing the score or soundtrack to a great movie . . . *your* movie. Your wedding!

Tutera Tip: As in the movies when there is no background music, a party without something in the background is a recipe for awkward silences. Background music should be playing at all times, throughout each section of your wedding: your ceremony, your cocktail hour, and your reception. Even if it is simply a CD of songs you and your groom love, it makes all the difference to your guests, whether they actively notice it or not (even during serious parts at your ceremony, the right selection can be an enhancement). Music is such a moving way to make a statement, to say more than just words and to convey what is important to you and what you are feeling on your day.

Ceremony Music

Consider using instrumentalists and vocalists for your overall ceremony music. Plan for their seating and for space in your ceremony, and ensure there are plentiful electrical outlets for them to use for music lamps, music stands, and electronically amplified instruments. Ceremony music can involve instrumentalists who are also in your reception band. Ideal instrumentalists for ceremony music are:

- Harpist
- Pianist
- Trio
- Guitarist
- Violinist
- Small string ensemble
- Vocalist

Song Selections

Start by choosing preceremony music, so your guests have something to listen to as they await your arrival. It's the beginning of your day, and music starts and creates the mood. For the entrance of your bridal party, choose something meaningful, like slowed adaptations of your favorite songs. Slower selections keep you and others from rushing down the aisle to the tempo.

Officiates, Grandparents, and Parents

You may choose to have a shortened version of an individual song for each of these members of the bridal party, or they can all walk down the aisle to the same song. Here are some suggested pieces:

- The Four Seasons—Antonio Vivaldi
- Adagio from Sonata in E-flat—Wolfgang Amadeus Mozart
- Air (from *Water Music*)—George Frederick Handel
- Air on the G String (from Orchestral Suite no. 3)—Johann Sebastian Bach
- Allegro from Brandenburg Concerto no. 4 in G—Bach
- Nocturne in E-flat, op. 9, no. 2—Frédéric Chopin
- Prelude to the Afternoon of a Faun—Claude Debussy

- Waltz (from *Sleeping Beauty*, act 1)—Pyotr Tchaikovsky
- "So This Is Love" (instrumental from the movie *Cinderella*)—Mack David, Al Hoffman, Jerry Livingston
- "The Rose"—Bette Midler
- "Only Time"—Enya
- "Come What May"—*Moulin Rouge* sound track
- "Fields of Gold"—Sting
- "Your Song"—Elton John

Bridal Party

Music for the entrance of your bridesmaids and groomsmen can be slightly more up-tempo or playful, both lyrically and in the nature of the song (pop ballads are more in line with your contemporaries than they would be for your officiant, grandparents, and parents).

- Canon in D Major—Johann Pachelbel
- "Jesu, Joy of Man's Desiring"—Johann Sebastian Bach
- "Angel Eyes"—Jim Brickman
- "In My Life" or "With a Little Help from My Friends"—The Beatles
- "I'll Be"—Edwin McCain
- "All My Life"—K-Ci and JoJo
- "When You Say Nothing At All"—Alison Krauss
- "Heaven" (Candlelight Mix)—DJ Sammy
- "I Honestly Love You"—Olivia Newton-John
- "Chasing Cars"—Snow Patrol
- "You and Me"—Lifehouse
- "You Light Up My Life"—LeAnn Rimes
- "Ave Maria"—Johann Sebastian Bach/Charles Gounod

Processional

Your processional music should be emotional, heartfelt, and tell everyone a story. I loved a ceremony where one of my brides descended a gorgeous church aisle to "I Believe in You and Me" sung by

Whitney Houston. Lyrically perfect for a wedding procession, the song was different than the expected bridal march but still extremely relevant. Another bride I worked with had an extremely emotional reason for choosing her song; as a tribute to her late father, she walked down the aisle to Josh Groban's "You Raise Me Up" (and there was not a dry eye in the house). From classical music to Broadway tunes to Italian opera or a Billboard ballad, your processional music is an integral part of the biggest statement you make all night.

- "(Everything I Do) I Do It For You"—Bryan Adams
- "Truly Madly Deeply"—Savage Garden
- "Kissing You" (theme from *William Shakespeare's Romeo + Juliet*)
- "At Last"—Etta James
- "When I Fall In Love"—Natalie Cole
- "Breathe"—Faith Hill
- "Musetta's Waltz" from *La Boheme*—Giacomo Puccini
- "Trumpet Voluntary"—Henry Purcell
- Toccata and Fuge in D Minor—Johann Sebastian Bach
- "When a Man Loves a Woman"—Percy Sledge

Special Music and Interludes

Music woven throughout enlivens your ceremony, continuously expresses emotion, and captures and keeps the attention of your guests. You may have a formal religious mass with songs sung by your congregation (which you can specially request) or perhaps you will have a vocalist, church choir, or other special instrumentalists to perform a song that has meaning to you. Music can be powerful as accompaniment to and dramatic emphasis on important occurrences in your ceremony (during the lighting of unity candles, prayers or meditations, religious happenings like Communion, and the breaking of the glass) or even as a separate performance on its own.

- "The Prayer"—Andrea Bocelli and Celine Dion
- "Come Away with Me"—Norah Jones

- "From This Moment"—Shania Twain
- "Through the Eyes of Love" (theme from *Ice Castles*)—Melissa Manchester
- "Wedding Song (There Is Love)"—Arranged by Richard Bradley
- "All I Ask of You"—from *The Phantom of the Opera* movie sound track
- "The Luckiest"—Ben Folds
- "Fly"—Sara Groves

Recessional

Your *very* first moments as bride and groom are something to celebrate, and the music as you exit your ceremony as husband and wife (finally!) should be just as jubilant as you feel! Select something uplifting with energy to reflect your joy and to raise your guests' spirits as you prepare to go to your reception and celebrate what they just witnessed.

- "Signed, Sealed, Delivered"—Stevie Wonder
- "This Will Be (An Everlasting Love)"—Natalie Cole
- "Hallelujah Chorus"—George Frederic Handel
- "Ode to Joy"—Ludwig von Beethoven
- "All You Need Is Love"—The Beatles
- "Thank You for Loving Me"—Bon Jovi
- "Oh Happy Day" (any version)
- "I Got You Babe"—Sonny and Cher
- "Love and Marriage"—Frank Sinatra

COCKTAIL AND RECEPTION MUSIC

Cocktail Hour Music

Having cocktail music sets a definitive mood for a brand-new segment of your wedding day, so make song selections that are light and upbeat! Keep the party flowing while allowing people to converse and mingle by hiring instrumentalists to play background music. As a good segue from your subdued ceremony music to a high-energy reception, bring in a pianist, trio, or singer, or have your DJ begin with some selections of jazz and classical, like Cole Porter, Stephen Sondheim, Duke Ellington, Frank Sinatra, Glen Miller, Nat King Cole, Ella Fitzgerald, Billie Holiday, George Gershwin, and Count Basie.

- "Fly Me to the Moon"—Frank Sinatra
- "Everything"—Michael Bublé
- "Let's Stay Together"—Al Green
- "I Say a Little Prayer for You"—Dionne Warwick
- "You're Just Too Good to Be True"—Frankie Valli

GENERAL TIPS ON THE SOUNDS OF YOUR SOIREE
- Music should escalate throughout the evening, with its style changing every thirty minutes.
- Sometimes there can be a fine line between chatterbox emcees and game-show hosts! If your DJ or band comes with an emcee, first see (and hear!) them in action, as nothing kills the flow (not to mention sophistication) of a party like emcees who like to get on the microphone and run a verbal marathon. Emcees should only speak when there are special announcements, not host your wedding like it's *The Newlywed Game*!
- Your dinner music should never be overpowering. Opt for light, soft background music with quiet vocals.

AND THE BAND PLAYED ON!: HIRING A BAND

Bands are the most tried-and-true form of energizing a room with song. Whether it's swing or salsa, a twenty-piece or a four-piece ensemble, live music has the ability to stir the soul of even the most stagnant chair-sitters at a reception!

Before you can find a band, you must first identify the style of music you want for your event. Think about what kind of sound you want. Is it tranquil, big band, contemporary, or great oldies? Choose specific sounds for each part of your wedding: ceremony, cocktail hour, and reception. Knowing what kind of moods you want to set for your guests will allow you to locate the band that is best suited for you. Remember that with entertainment, the possibilities are endless; there is definitely something for everyone. Choosing the right band is more than just choosing people to play your first dance—choosing the right band is about finding a way to show off your style, highlight your personalities, and ensure your guests have an enjoyable time. Some bands can vary in style, and others specialize in one type of music, so know what you want, then audition bands to find the right one.

If you're going to be paying for a band, you might as well have one that "fits" the bill! Discuss appropriate attire with your band leader. Many bands come with costuming you can select from, from formal to funky, so work with them to perpetuate the overall look and feel of your wedding. If you have a formal wedding, request the black-tie ensemble, but if you are going in a different direction, know that not all bands have to wear tuxedos, and they will likely dress to accommodate your party's look.

"Seeing" is not necessarily "believing" when it comes to bands! Seek out your band with your ears and never hire a band you have not heard play live firsthand. Ask your potential musicians if you can see them perform; hearing a CD or seeing a video is not enough! Ask for references and see for yourself so you are certain and comfortable with your choice. This is one of the most important tasks of planning your wedding. Do this together as bride and groom, give yourself time, and have fun!

It is crucial that you choose a playlist with your band. Give your band any songs you particularly want to hear, including your special

dance songs, as early in advance as possible. (If it's of utmost importance to you to have a band play "your" song, make sure they are willing to learn it before you sign with them!) A "Do Not Play" list is just
as, if not more, important than a playlist! "Y.M.C.A.," "Macarena,"
and "The Electric Slide" are no-no's (and you know it).

GUIDELINES TO GIVE YOUR BAND

- Provide them with a call time that allows them enough
  time to arrive, unload, set up, and tune their instruments.
  Make sure to give them very clear directions to get them to
  the right place—you don't want to deal with a lost band on
  the day of your wedding! Music is too pertinent to even
  risk it!

- The day of the wedding, a point person needs to cue the
  band during your event (especially during your ceremony)
  to notify them when and when not to play. In your prewedding meetings with your band, you should go over your
  timeline and details with them, but having someone on
  hand the day of is of value to both you and the performers.

I DO's for Choosing a Band

- Get references from wedding couples, not corporate clients
  or even birthday party clients. A wedding has very specific
  needs and ways of entertaining. Ask other couples for their
  favorite parts, what they liked and what they disliked.

- Make sure what you see is what you get. When you are watching your band live, if you fall in love with any part of it (from
  backup singers to lead singers), make precise requests for it
  in your contract.

- If a band won't or can't learn "your song," play the actual
  CD of the song instead. (In fact, it will sound much better
  than a poor version done by the band.) For songs that are
  cultural or should just sound a certain way, also do not hesitate to skip the band on them. A swing band singing Bryan

Adams or a Jamaican steel drum band playing the hora just *might* not cut it.

- With both your band and your venue, coordinate the setup time for the band to arrive and do their sound check. Make sure everyone is on the same page, with the same cues of when (and when not) to go on.

- Make sure your venue has proper power for the electrical needs of your band and entertainment. There should be no blackouts!

- Give the band leader your wedding timeline. Wedding bands work with events very often, but it is important to go over with them the key parts of yours and any important moments. Meet to discuss your timeline a week or two prior to your wedding (not too early, as they have other weddings and events that you do not want them to confuse with yours). These coordination meetings are not to be missed primarily because you, the bride, should not be running the show and worrying about anything except having the time of your life!

- Know that bands come with a rider, a list of all the requirements a band has that you are responsible for providing or accommodating upon hiring them and signing a contract. Riders either serve as your contract or are a supplement to what you will be signing, and include all the smallest details, like what foods a band may require, what size their stage should be, how much space they need in a greenroom (preparation room), how much time they need to set up, what technicians they must use, and/or what sound and lighting stipulations come with them. Water and food are sometimes left up to you as the client to provide, and sometimes your caterer will include band meals or the rider will include meals in the cost—just make sure you plan this beforehand and read carefully!

- Bands will need breaks and break rooms, (this is also usually specified in their rider), so ask if your band will be taking breaks in shifts to keep the momentum going. It is in your best interest to insist breaks are in sections so there is always live music playing: no silences ever! ("Break" cannot mean "no music"!) Inform them they are to go to the break area, not sit on the side of the stage or hang out in the guest area (or at the bar!).

- Raise the band up on a platform so you and your guests can see them and so they have a look of professionalism and command the attention of your guests and encourage them to party!

- Make sure your bandleader can correctly *pro-nounce* your bridal party names (and the names of other family members that will be announced: anyone giving toasts, anyone being introduced, anyone doing special dances). Your bandleader needs to know you and feel connected to you so you are not just another number. Provide for them a written phonetic spelling of your names.

- Find out the band's stage requirements and the size of the stage you need to accommodate them—and make sure you can even fit them before you hire them! Discuss with your band the size of the stage they will need, and make sure the venue and the band will be able to work together. No sense in paying for a huge band if the venue will not fit them!

- Light the band and the dance floor. It is so important that everyone can see the band and the floor you and your guests are dancing on. It will also encourage people to participate—no one is drawn to a dark dance floor.

- Some bands provide a lighting package in their services; however, oftentimes it's not attractive, so beware and ask questions. It may be better to source out the lighting of the band to a lighting professional. Keep your band out of the dark and from looking like an early nineties concert by using soft washes to illuminate the performers. If the band comes with their own great lighting professional, their performance and the lighting of your room need to all be coordinated with your venue and its lighting team. If there is just one lighting company that is working with both the band and your venue, make sure they are in communication with your entertainers regarding the band's needs like spotlighting and the proper staging look.

I DON'Ts for Choosing a Band

- Avoid having only one style of music throughout. As much as you and your groom might love the Rolling Stones, not everyone else necessarily will . . . which is why you need to appeal to everyone all night. This also encourages more than one group of people with a certain taste to dance!
- Don't rely on only CDs and DVDs when you're choosing a band. You must see the bands in person to get to know their energy live, and to truly see how they look and how they react to one another.
- Don't be too kitschy with the look of your band—it is still a wedding, not a prom or a high school production!
- When plotting out your room, don't position a band or entertainment group too far from your dance floor. They must be directly in front of the guests or floor; otherwise there is a "disconnect" and the room's energy falls.
- Please don't make the mistake of hiring a band you saw at a bar or in an outdoor concert. While they may be the best band in the world, the sound requirements, performance techniques, and technical details are much different in a wedding event venue. As much as you dig their sound, a fun backyard rock band you found at an alternative music fes-

tival that you can sign just by writing your number and wedding date on a cocktail napkin poses many potential problems! Hire a professional band that enables you to be contractually protected and that is prepared to perform proficiently in front of all your guests.

SPIN MY SONG: HIRING A DJ

Disc jockeys (DJs) are an excellent choice and much less expensive than live entertainment. Many of my brides lean toward using DJs because the playlist can be specifically customized to suit their wishes. Although DJs used to be associated with parties for younger crowds, this is no longer the case; a well-chosen, sophisticated DJ can be just the right entertainment for a wedding.

If your venue provides an in-house DJ for a reasonable price, don't just take the venue's word that they are the right DJ for you. When finding a DJ, contact local entertainment companies that specialize in providing entertainers for weddings. Ask for a list of the types of parties (the list must include weddings) the DJ has worked. Meet the DJ to learn about his or her personality and style. Discuss your needs and wishes for your wedding, including the DJ's wardrobe. Whether in-house or outsourced, watch the DJ in action (ask if you can see him or her play during another wedding—but don't be wedding crashers, now!). Listen to him or her spin and mix in action to see if you are comfortable first.

When meeting with your DJ, be sure to sit down and talk about various styles of music. One of the biggest benefits of having a DJ is that they intermingle the various generations of guests' musical tastes that otherwise wouldn't be covered by a single-sound band. A variety should be played throughout the night to keep all your guests interested and the mood ever changing!

That said, spend time developing your song playlist. During your meetings with your DJ, have him or her provide you with a list of song styles. Highlight and strike through what you do and do not want to hear. (The last thing you want to deal with is a song that reminds you of an ex-boyfriend blaring through the speakers on your special day with your new man!) Make sure your DJ will take your song requests; many just need the title and artist, and they will add your preferences.

When bringing in your own DJ, ensure that he/she has the right sound equipment. DJs either bring their own sound systems or can sometimes use the venue's house system. For receptions, I strongly recommend your DJ bring the right equipment to be amplified and *not* rely on your venue's house system, but if just for the cocktail hour, light background music through a house system is usually fine.

> *Tutera Tip: Be wary of your DJ's physical setup and standard lighting accessories. Ask how your DJ decorates his or her platform and equipment: It's your wedding, not a roller rink, which means no disco balls, no 1980s lighting, and no rope lights or Christmas lights allowed! If you like your DJ's style and personality but not his or her choice of decor, ask for the accent pieces to be left at home and go for a simple, discreet setup.*

A SWEET DUET:
DJS WITH ACCOMPANIMENT

There's something about hearing your favorite song the way it was famously done by the original artist, yet there's also an exciting energy about live music that many brides gravitate toward. Perhaps a combination of both is how you want to get your guests on their feet. If hiring a full band or orchestra is beyond your budget, a great alternative is to hire a DJ who also has a few instrumentalists that play with the music for a more robust, interactive sound. Keep the familiar sound of favorite recorded songs and add something special with one of these live instruments:

- Saxophones
- Electric strings
- Percussion instruments
- Bongo drums
- Electric pianos

You also may consider hiring performers on a smaller scale: A single amplified guitarist can set the entire audible ambience at a ceremony, or a few local musicians can liven up any reception. Or choosing a shorter session for your band and ending the night with a DJ may be just the right happy medium (happy for your guests, happy for your budget, happy for you!).

SHOWSTOPPERS: HIRING PERFORMERS

Performance entertainment has such a wide range that it needs to be selected with care. Think deeply about your personality, your style as a couple, what you love, and what entertains you. If any of those things would easily translate to mass entertainment and continue to tell your story as a couple to your guests, it may be a great way to add some personal creativity, fun, and flair to your wedding. One of my brides had a gospel choir sing her favorite song, "Oh Happy Day," and it brought down the house. To me, anything that keeps your guests delighted, surprised, guessing, and unable to forget your wedding is good entertainment.

Entertainment is also a great arena to play up your heritage. For a Scottish wedding, I hired a bagpiper to play as the guests exited the ceremony. One of my Indian brides hired authentic henna tattoo artists. Another bride and groom did a Thai water ceremony set to music during their vow exchange and created a memorable and beautiful sight for everyone to witness. Infusing religion or culture is great to emphasize who you are, and to make your wedding more of your story.

Other special performances during your reception can be entertaining and sentimental, showstopping or subtle. Perhaps you and your sweetheart met at college, and a soft instrumental version of your alma mater is played by a violinist during your cocktail party. Or perhaps your fiancé won you over in a grand display of affection where a song dedication and the retelling of the story would only do it justice. Have fun with your entertainment and in creating the "sound track" to your wedding story. Here are some suggested performers to hire to incorporate special or heritage music:

- Pianists
- Violinists
- Opera singers
- Strolling cultural musicians
- Trios or quartets
- Groupings of vocalists

Entertainment is a way that, through participation or observation, everyone can get involved. The possibilities go on and on, and the best part is that they are entirely dependent on how you choose to make your special day more like you.

GOING OUT WITH A BANG: WEDDING FIREWORKS

A nighttime ceremony simply beckons for a magical touch of romance. Even just a spark or two of light in the sky can be an awe-inspiring moment for your guests that will make your wedding out of the ordinary and over-the-top. If you are to be wed in a location where fireworks can be set off, read on regarding the process, the budgeting, and the options you have for a love that lights up the sky.

For a fireworks display, whether it's as simple as just a few sparks or as elaborate as a full show, there are just a few more steps than going out into your backyard, setting off a bottle rocket, and running for cover. Always hire a professional company through an entertainment company or choose one that has worked in the town of your wedding venue before (often, there are not many so they should be relatively easy to find).

Ask about specifics when contracting pyrotechnic artists. Like all vendors, by describing to them your style, colors, and venue, they may have some great suggestions for you. Decide with them (in full detail) the type of fireworks that will be detonated, from colors and appearance to sound and height. Ask them for a wedding-specific show. Pyrotechnics can match the color scheme of your wedding, can be in gold and silver shimmers, or even can explode in heart shapes.

Also select with your company the ideal timing of your show. My favorites are:

- As you say "I do"
- As you cut your cake
- As you move to a different location
- As you and your groom drive away from either the ceremony or the reception
- As a great photo opportunity

Tutera Tip: Because fireworks come with abrupt sounds and bright lights, think through how they play into your entire wedding scenario. (For example, if you have horses waiting to take you away in a carriage under a sky lit with color, your horses will need to be far enough from the sound that they will not get spooked.) Share

your timeline and your wedding details with your fireworks
contact for professional advisement.

Any fireworks display must comply with sound ordinances, with a detonation range, and with fire marshals (and must be legal in your state)! The company you contract will handle all of this for you, and by doing so, this ensures they are liable (and not you!), but it is in your best interest to make sure this is on their to-do list. Find a pyrotechnic company early, so if any of these scenarios pose a problem, you have enough time to rationally, calmly, and effectively find a new solution before you are locked into a payment for goods that cannot be delivered.

Determining Fireworks Cost Without Torching Your Budget

The cost of a fireworks display depends on how big a production you do, as well as what state or location you are in (rural Virginia versus New York City is going to be a significant cost difference!).

You may not even need to spend a lot of money on the fireworks if you just need a few to be set off. The length of a show also determines how much you will spend; the amount of fireworks you blow up is directly proportional with the cost you pay. (Don't do a thirty-minute show. It's not the Fourth of July; you're celebrating your union, not your independence!) Avoid restless guests and keep fireworks to ten minutes or less. It's a moment to make a dramatic statement (or exit!) that should be just that—a moment.

If a sparkling sky show isn't in your budget but you just can't bear to rule out exiting in a blaze of glory, know that fireworks are not necessarily the big spectacles that you see in the sky . . . they can be big spectacles on the ground with a lighted free-standing construction of your monogram. Grounded fireworks can make a statement that is simple but still has a lot of pizzazz. And always remember: The safety of your guests should be the number-one priority for every bride-to-be.

MUSIC PLANNER WORKSHEET

Ceremony Music			
	Songs	Performed By	Start Time
Prelude			
Processional			
Ceremony			
Recessional			

Reception Music			
	Song	Performed By	Start Time
Cocktail Hour			
Couple's First Dance			
Father/Daughter Dance			
Mother/Son Dance			
Dinner			
Dancing			
Cake-Cutting			

(continued)

Reception Music			
	Song	Performed By	Start Time
Other Special Requests			
Don't-Play List			

Other			
	Song	Performed By	Start Time
Announcements, Dedications, and Toasts			

Eight

LIGHTS, CAMERA, ACTION!: PHOTOGRAPHY AND VIDEOGRAPHY

YOUR PERSONAL PAPARAZZI: HIRING A PHOTOGRAPHER

What is it about an event that makes it so much more exciting when there are camera crews and photographers clamoring to immortalize it with photos and footage? It's the fact that there's something so spectacular going on that it's worth all that effort to capture it forever. . . . Your wedding day is going to be such a spectacular event in its own right that you'll of course want to hold on to it as long as possible—which is why it's so important for you to find the perfect photographer to give you the perfect photo that will show all the inquiring minds what a beautiful wedding you had, and remind you of every detail years from now! (There's a reason the paparazzi have jobs. . . .) On your wedding day, it's your time to shine at your red-carpet event, so choosing your photographer and videographer is also choosing the best ways to document lifetime memories . . . starring you.

It's extremely important that you like your photographer. *A lot.* You're going to be spending the *most* time of your wedding with your photographer (so while you think you need to like people like your wedding planner, even more than that, you need to *love* your photographer . . . well, maybe not more than me, your "other" man!). It's a must for you to feel comfortable with your photographer and have him or her become your best friend for the day . . . because on that day, your photographer is going to be with you every moment: while you're getting dressed, hugging your mom, crying (tears of joy and hopefully not anything else), having a bridezilla moment (did I say that?). . . . Your photographer will see every emotion of yours in those twenty-four hours. The last thing you want to add to all that is any sense of discomfort with the person behind the camera capturing it all. The only way to find out who the right person is to fill that role is by spending time meeting with various photographers: Get to know them and allow them to get to know you in your meetings, and never simply rely on the quality of work in their portfolios or what you've seen online.

Overall, photographers and videographers can be simple point-and-shoot clickers or true visionary artists. Ask to see their work and honestly discuss with them what styles of work they have already done and which of those styles you prefer. Go over a shot list with them that includes all the photos and footage you want (including the scene of all the bridesmaids sticking their fancy shoes in a circle together) and all the ones you don't want (including cousin Frank falling down next to the bar after one too many "specialty cocktails").

Copy That: Photography Copyrights

Often, photographers are viewed as artists, and the photographs they take of your wedding are theirs, by right. They own the images (and you just buy prints of them). Think of it as if they are the creators of paintings or any other type of art—it's their work, and if you like it, you can purchase it from them but not always take credit for it. Some photographers (rarely, but it's plausible) will negotiate giving the rights to you, to duplicate and manipulate as you please, but others require you to pay per print and ask permission for publishing. Check with your photographer what their copyrights are and make sure you are comfortable with their policy before signing.

Know what is included in your photography package and what you will have to purchase after the wedding. Make sure prior to signing your contract that you clearly understand what you get. When someone is charging you, what are you receiving? Ask about quantity, quality, image sizes, and copyrighting. It may be extremely tedious, but you have to make sure you are not going to be surprised after the wedding if you are charged for photos you assumed would be yours. When it comes to wanting things included and signing a deal, don't assume anything and ask your photographer to educate you.

Tutera Tip: Before you sign your contract, inquire about the styles in which the photographer can print your photo album. Ask to see samples. These styles will also vary in price, so review all the upgrades up front so you aren't tempted later.

Part of what will make the right photographer truly the right photographer is when your styles (in addition to personalities) are in line. Discuss what each potential photographer's "shooting style" is and go through his or her work to find what style (or multiple styles) will best depict your wedding in the ways you will want to remember it forever.

YOUR DEFINING MOMENT: A PHOTOGRAPHY STYLES GLOSSARY

Portraiture/Portrait Photography. The facial expression of anyone in the photo is predominant. Like mood music and mood lighting . . . this is mood photography! For example: The focus of a bridal portrait would be your emotion portrayed by the look on your face (or the look on the face of you with your groom, you with your flower girl, you with your father . . .). This is not a snapshot of people conveying an emotion, but more a still shot, purposefully posed.

Posed. Like portraiture, this style is a planned, crafted photograph look, but with less artistry and more strategic placing of people. A family portrait would often be like this (not so much to portray mood and expression like in portraiture, but to deliberately get certain shots). A good example: a photo of the joined newlyweds and their families at the altar.

Candid Style. This is the style of unposed, spontaneous moments! These are "snapshots" but also can be very telling, poignant, and beautiful through capturing the subject (your flower girl dancing, you midlaugh, your brothers hugging) through the art of being "in the moment." Interactions, natural emotions, memories . . . candids are a great way to remember your wedding day exactly the way it occurred.

Journalistic Style/Photojournalism. This is the style that thrives on "storytelling" through the capture and presentation of photographs in an order that's timely and narrative. (These photos are not just of you, but also of your rings, of your ceremony space, of your shoes, of your bouquet lying on its side. . . .) Photojournalism silently leads the viewer through your event.

I DO's for Hiring a Photographer

- Ask for references! A good photographer (and vendor in general) will be happy to provide you with a list of references or letters of recommendation from past clients. Also do your own research and ask around (and use the Internet to your advantage to get in touch with past brides) about your photographer's reputation, personality, and style.

- Meet with your photographer to plan out when you should take your wedding photos—before, during, or after your ceremony. By taking all your photos before the wedding day, you get all the shots you want without rushing around. You prevent yourself from losing valuable time at your ceremony or cocktail hour that shouldn't be spent looking for people and posing for hundreds of shots! (Instead, you can take your time and have fun.) While you forgo the tradition of "not seeing each other before the ceremony," overriding it may be worth being able to calmly take all the pictures you need and still spend time with your guests, but that is a personal choice you need to make. If you decide to stay with tradition, just make sure you have alloted time in your schedule for picture taking and don't mind missing cocktails, so you are not rushed!

- Think about the photographer's timeline, not just your own. In wedding reality, you can't hold up the schedule of your wedding and the event flow, but you do want to think of the time you need to take the photos you want to get. Plan out what photos you can take ahead of time. If you are taking some posed the day of, plot out what shots should happen where and when. When you sit down with your photographer, make a shooting schedule that coincides with your production schedule. You have to leave enough time for the photographer to do their job—even Annie Leibovitz needs a reasonable amount of time to work her magic!

Allow travel time for you and your photographer to get to various locations.

- When selecting your specific photo scenes, put your ideas all together and make a plan to efficiently get them all in. Don't lose time by jumping all over town as you think of photo shoot locations off the top of your head . . . that would only make you exhausted! Keep your list simple so you don't look tired by the time you do your first dance!

- Your photographer should provide you with a detailed shot list to review. Make sure it includes everything you and your family want (and notes what you *don't* want!). Mentally walk through each segment of your wedding (starting with preceremony and ending with your reception departure) when adding in the special details you'd like shot. Discuss highlights of your wedding your photographer may not be aware of so nothing goes uncaptured—remember, you only get one "shot" to get it all in!

Tutera Tip: You should never be chasing and looking for those you want in your pictures. The photographer, a friend, a family member, or a bridal party member should assist in this task.

- Look into different finishes and special effects for your photos, from sepia tones to black-and-white prints, artistic colorings, and more. I'm not a big believer in manipulating photos too much because it takes away from the realism of your wedding, but it can't hurt to ask what the photographer can do to make your photos unique. Look at samples of all these possibilities to help define your taste.

YOUR DEFINING MOMENT: A PHOTO FINISHES GLOSSARY

Glossy. A smooth, shiny coating on paper: like a mirrored surface. Glossy photos yield the richest colors and the sharpest contrasts.

Lustre. A smooth surface that is less reflective than glossy, but still resists fingerprints. This is the finish used most commonly by professionals.

Matte. A coated, no-shine finish. Colors appear softer and there is a dullness (yet still high-quality resolution) to the photos.

Watercolor. A printing style that makes photos look as if they were painted in watercolor. Sharpness and definition is replaced by gentle strokes and blurring of lines, resulting in a more artistic (less photographic) rendition of your photo. You are still able to define facial features and details of your photos, and these prints are often mounted on canvas.

- Ask the photographer if her or she is shooting in digital or film. (That alone says a lot about the photographer's style.) Digital gives more opportunities to manipulate the photos (you can change the lighting, coloring, exposure, textures, sharpening, saturation, and—everyone's best friends—airbrushing and retouching).
- Ask your photographer if he or she will post all your photos online after your wedding to enable friends and family to purchase them from the Web site. (This isn't something you want to spend your time doing, whether it is uploading the hundreds of shots yourself or keeping track of which aunt wanted which photo of you with which cousins.) Find out how long they will be online and other details such as whether you can edit them on the Web site or simply just place orders.
- Have an engagement photo session. You will definitely find an opportunity to use your best shots at your wedding, and it's a good trial run to get you comfortable both with you photographer and with yourself in front of the lens.

Tutera Tip: *Many brides want to place disposable cameras on the table to enable their guests to take photos. If you do this, do it with style! Customize the cameras to match your wedding decor, and instead of preplacing them on the tables, have them brought out by waiters a half hour into the reception (simply putting them out makes the tables look messy). Having them "served" makes them an event on the timeline and adds to the "something different every thirty minutes" philosophy. Add a cute note that invites guests to take photos instead of dumping each camera on the table and implying that they should: Something even as simple as "Smile! You're at Samantha and Andrew's wedding!" Send your disposable cameras to your photographer to add to the album.*

I DON'Ts for Wedding Photography

- Don't be surprised by who you end up with as a photographer! If you're going into a large photography house and they have twenty different shooters, make sure you're not just hiring the name of the company but the exact person you want for your wedding. If you go to a big studio, ensure they state in your contract that you're shooting with the same person you think you are. (If you fall in love with photos from an album, make sure that you will be getting the very photographer you know is capable of providing you with the similar result!)

- After the wedding, bar yourself from wielding the "magic" retouching wand too much, no matter now tempted you are! It's the same concept as with your makeup: Don't go overboard on changing your physical appearance, or in five years when you look back at your photos, you won't even recognize your beautiful self! Though a little airbrushing never hurt anybody (amen!), it's important that your photos still look like you when all is said and done.

- Don't have your photographer take table group shots. Anyone can do those—use your photographer as a more artistic resource.

- Don't feel uncomfortable in front of the camera! Though it's a fact that you are going to look gorgeous, being in front of a camera for hours on end can be daunting for even the bravest of brides. Get familiar with how it feels to be the center of the camera's attention and spend some time with your fiancé taking pictures of each other for fun. Look at what photos you like of yourself to learn what poses you feel good about, and what expressions look best, so when you get your real wedding photos back, you aren't wishing you "didn't make that face" or "stand that way"! Practice makes perfect. Know how to position your head, where to put your arms, what stance you think is most flattering for you, and what facial movements you like and don't like, and perfect the various smiles you will be flashing for the camera on your big day!

ROLL THE CAMERAS!: HIRING A VIDEOGRAPHER

Capturing memories on film is something that you can only do once, and they become only more and more valuable over time. I am a huge advocate of hiring a great videographer for the sole purpose of having that live footage you can never create—your grandma dancing up a storm with your nieces and nephews, the sound of people's voices and laughter at your dinner . . . your first dance and the facial expressions that went along with every special moment. If you can make the budget work, you will be thankful in the end.

Start selecting your videographer based upon who has the best equipment. Selecting this particular vendor is something you must do with an eye for quality in order to get your money's worth.

Don't hire a videographer who has lots of video equipment—in this case, bigger is not better! Bright lights, sound equipment, umbrellas, and poles are fine for a press conference but not for your wedding! Find a videographer who knows how to film weddings (not press conferences) and who truly understands the power of memories caught on tape . . . memories that are real and spontaneous (the best kind!).

Look at the videographer's work and make sure it's compatible to who you are as a couple, and that the style of the filming (and even more important, the editing) fits your personality. Take advantage of having your night recorded on digital film. Videography tells a very different story than photography does, and there's so much more you can do with technology because of the movement. A four-minute highlight video set to music can capture the evening and make people truly feel as if they were there (or as if they were there again!).

Ask your videographer about your options for videography styles. Don't just read about styles—view samples of what they look like to find out what works best for you.

YOUR DEFINING MOMENT: A VIDEOGRAPHY STYLES GLOSSARY

Reality. Filmed just as it happened, with the audio of conversation and with optional background music.

No Sound. Filmed with sound edited out, possibly with slow-motion effects and entirely backed by a music sound track.

Documentary. Like an interview; the bride and groom have some moments speaking directly to or near the camera eye, with narratives and voice-overs (does not have to be the entire duration, can be cuts within a larger reality or no-sound video).

Combination. If you find yourself liking multiple styles, do a little of each style in one video—have your cake and eat it, too!

Take the time to pick out great music with your videographer: The perfectly placed song playing during your video can make all the difference to the viewer.

Speak with your videographer about special effects: slow motion, text, fades, and other videography editing tricks can be the defining line between classy and cheesy. If edits and special effects are done well, they can elevate the quality of the video to an over-the-top perfect wedding memory, so ask about options when it comes to postproduction of your footage.

And That's a Wrap: Fun Ways to Edit and Show Your Video

Now, more than ever, videographers can use their gadgets and gizmos to do amazing things on amazingly quick timelines.

For example, in an "instant edit," the footage your videographer takes that very night is edited into a short clip a few minutes long of the evening's events. It is then copied onto DVDs and packaged up in favor boxes just in time for your guests to take home a memento of their night. Your guests will be amazed and get to relive their special moments with you right away.

For one of my brides, I did a fabulous videography favor. She gave a DVD of the wedding (that enabled the guest to choose to watch either a four-minute or a twenty-minute version) packaged in a lavender box that complemented the wedding design, and sent it out with her thank-you notes. This could be a simple way to say thank you for your gift and/or for celebrating with you. It's even a nice notion to send your DVD out to your guests on your one-year anniversary, just for the sake of remembering the fun times had!

Save costs by having your videographer and photographer be from the same company (and possibly be a package deal). Beware of finding a company that has artists in different arenas though—do your homework to make sure you are getting the best skilled vendors no matter where they are from or if they are independent or not.

If you so choose, have a video montage. Work with a videographer a few months before your wedding to compile a lovely five-minute (or shorter) creative compilation of photos, footage, comments from both you and the groom about how you met, and anything more you want to include to help tell "your story" to your guests. Whatever you do . . . *don't* play a twenty-five minute slide show of photos that requires your guests to stand around and appropriately comment "How cute!" Title it something to define its purpose, like "The Joining of Two" or "The Perfect Combination," and then keep it to a minimum. The ideal timeline for a montage:

0:00–1:00 minutes—Bride growing up
1:00–2:00 minutes—Groom growing up
2:00–4:00 minutes—Photos of you together as a couple up
until the day of the wedding

Whether to be shown at your wedding or every year after, a beautifully done video is multipurpose. Video can share a side of your relationship your guests may not really know and lead them through a narrative of how you got to your big day . . . or serve as your truest form of keeping your wedding memories retrievable for the rest of your life. The perspective of your videographer can creatively and emotionally immortalize these moments of your life. Remember, your wedding is your story, and photographs and videos illustrate that story for a lifetime.

Nine

ORDINARY TO EXTRAORDINARY: YOUR WEDDING DECOR

Finally, the part of the wedding where you get to make the visual part of how you picture the affair come to life! I find that decor is what gets my brides most excited and eager to plan their weddings. It's also, for me, the main reason I love my job as a designer and planner as much as I do. Decor allows me to take my brides and all their guests to a place that previously they could experience only in their imagination. Now you're about to take that fantasy wedding scene and turn it into your actual wedding ceremony, cocktail party, and reception. This is the part, as they say, where all the magic happens.

This chapter is titled "Ordinary to Extraordinary" with valid reason: Wedding decor begins with an *ordinary* place and takes you through a creative adventure resulting in an *extraordinary* wedding with enchanting, unforgettable surroundings. Decor, among your other elements, is the main way you transport your guests to another place and time where belief is suspended.

Decor brings your personality to life by enabling you to convey who you are and what experience you want your guests to have while with you. It's very personal . . . and also very, very enjoyable! Choosing the decor should be the most fun any bride has when planning her wedding—it's all looks and inspired by hopes and dreams. Every decision is more exciting than the last, and they all lead up to one aesthetically beautiful and captivating scenario in which the best moments of your life among family and friends will take place. It's like creating your own once-in-a-lifetime wonderland that stems from things you love.

And that's where I come in. My job is to meet with my bridal clients (and through this book—that's you!) to find out exactly what you want and to show you how to get it. Being a good wedding designer is like being a good translator—I take what I hear from you, and accurately create it out of the language of art.

Creating an atmosphere for your event is easier than you might think. The atmosphere is a culmination of the following elements: style, flowers, table design, and lighting. Each of these is part of the overall picture.

DESIGNING YOUR DREAM: CONTRACTING A DESIGN VENDOR

When meeting with a design vendor (a floral company, a draping company, or anyone who is providing you with decorative elements), make sure you get a design presentation before you give your "okay" with a plan. You have to see what you're going to get. In my office, for each client I stage a "demo" where the client comes in and I do an entire example table for them. This stage is crucial for both my company and my clients to make sure everyone is on the same page.

Sometimes things appear different than they were written or conceptualized. It's during this presentation that changes are made and perhaps new ideas are discussed. In some cases, designers can turn out to cause more wedding stress and more wedding work than you expect (move over, mother-in-law!), so make sure you find a design vendor that understands you, respects your ideas, and wants to work as your partner to create something special for you.

When I meet with my brides and grooms, I first find out as much as I possibly can about what makes them tick—what makes them happy, what makes them *them*. I ask a *lot* of questions to find answers that will, in the end, all combine and equate to their overall wedding style.

The moral of the "discover who you are" story is this: I help my brides take all their ideas, dreams, and visions and make them make sense and become tangible to them. In this chapter, I'm going to help you discover who you are so you can properly communicate with your own designer to make sure you are getting the day you dreamed of! First we need to find out what your bridal style is—not what your personal style is in life. (You may like to set up your house with one look and you may like to dress in another—these could hint at what your wedding style is, but your wedding style itself is completely different. Who's to say that a straightlaced business lady in a three-button suit doesn't want to be a princess on the one day she's a bride?) Your wedding style is just your wedding style—it can be anything you want it to be, and this is all about personal choice and your personal preference!

I once had a bride who told me, "I know exactly what kind of wedding I want! I'm such a classic bride." When she started to explain to me the kinds of things she wanted and then showed me photos of things I had done that she liked, it turned out that she was actually not classic at all—she always chose styles that were modern! It's easy to transpose words that to one person mean one thing and to another mean something entirely different (there's that translator part again—can we say "language barrier"?), so let's make sure you are using the right words to identify yourself.

WHAT'S YOUR BRIDAL STYLE?

One of a wedding planner's first questions is "What kind of bride are you and what wedding style do you have?" When we ask that, we're not trying to find out what kind of *person* you are or what kind of *style* you have in your life. Remember, your bridal and wedding wants can be entirely different from your everyday persona. Read the descriptions twice: once with your ceremony in mind, and then again thinking about your reception. Happy self-discovery!

The Classic Bride: Traditional Elegance

This bride loves regality, the picturesque wedding made of girlhood dreams. From everything white to soft pastels, the classic bride chooses colors that are timeless, elegant, rich, ethereal, and romantic. Grand opulence is a must: candelabras with tall taper candles and explosions of flowers—lots of flowers (for instance, white roses)—and the use of gold or silver and dripping crystals. Endless candles of all sizes, and low crystal or precious metal containers with flowers (like roses, peonies, lilies, and hydrangea) might decorate her tables. Luxurious linens, chandeliers, and ornate detailing and sparkling jewels abound. The classic bride is elaborate and traditional to a "T."

The Modern Bride: Sophisticated Edge

The modern bride gravitates toward chic, sleek, and sophisticated lines. Visually appealing, dynamic, and trendy, her wedding will be as fashion-forward as she is. Clean and loungy with a bit of an edge, modern decor includes gleaming, contemporary lines and clear, reflective surfaces like glass and Lucite to create illusion and shape. Orchids, tulips, and calla lilies in containers with edges or sheen bring out the beauty of form and function. Ideal for a young and hip bride, this sexy style is best illustrated with smooth and glossy finishes and shimmery metallics, and has an overall pristine look.

The Eclectic Bride: Dramatic Fun

The eclectic bride is pure dramatic fun—hip and funky, and up for anything. The wedding itself reflects her bold and dramatic personality with elements that are totally unexpected but totally fabulous. By adding splashes of dramatic colors, the eclectic bride makes her surroundings look alive, and lets people know they are in a wedding scene unlike any other. A deliberate mixture of bohemian patterns and textures, from fabrics to feathers, combine to make out-of-the-box extravagance. Interesting containers, irregularly shaped blooms (like orchids) and unique foliage (like branches) capture this bride's essence. Avant-garde with an invigorating vibe, an eclectic wedding is as full of life and as unrepeatable as they come, just like the bride.

The Garden Bride: Refreshing Whimsy

In the sweet, fresh serenity of a whimsical garden scene, the garden bride has a playful, naturally beautiful, and romantic persona. A garden wedding makes a statement without making an obvious scene—the surroundings of colorful blossoming flowers and beautiful greens create a surreal setting, perfect to be married in. A garden bride leans toward the use of floral topiaries, chiffon and sheer fabrics, wrought iron, rustic urns, and sun-drenched grasses. Butterfly accents and rich velvety moss create the magic of an enchanted garden. The garden bride likes romance, prettiness, and peacefulness. Light and airy materials, and the sweet aroma and harmony of the outdoors, create a gentle and comforting sense of love for the garden bride.

Which did you turn out to be? Your answer may have been what you always thought you were, and if it was something different than you expected, you're now ready to go forth and speak the designer language to get what you want!

Not all brides are a clear-cut style—that's why it's style! It's all about who *you* are! If you often found yourself between two answers, you just might be a combination. You can absolutely cross styles to make one that's your own, or incorporate more than one (in fact, that's one of my favorite things to do). Once I had a bride who had a very traditional wedding: extremely sedate and very proper . . . only to then have one of the funkiest receptions I had ever seen, full of color, modern pieces, and all kinds of shapes and abstracts used in her floral designs. This was quite a hit with the guests, who were delighted with the surprise of being at a wedding that was the best of both worlds!

Tutera Tip: To make sure you and your designer are on the same page (literally!), bring clippings from magazines, examples from movies, descriptions from books, photos of flowers and arrangements, pictures of inspirational buildings, or anything else that visually moves you and is what you want for your wedding. Listen very carefully to how you describe what you want, and then back it up with photos to make sure it makes sense and that everyone is speaking the same design language!

Once you settle in on the style, then it is time to talk about the overall colors. Style first, then color: These both are of the utmost importance to decide before we do anything else designwise.

Color Me Beautiful

The wedding colors you choose will also say a great deal about what your big event will look like. Wedding colors can set a mood based on color selection alone. An all-white wedding creates a separate image from even a collection of pastels. Deep sunset colors are far different from bold primaries. You may even be looking at designer colors, like a chocolate brown paired with a cool ice blue, or a bold orange with white, soft peach and subtle green, to make a unique yet elegant combination. Look around you to see what colors strike you pleasantly. Choose from Pantone color wheels to hone in on the exact shade. Those you choose will be woven throughout every element of your wedding, so look far and wide and fall deeply in love with your colors!

Once you and your designer find out the colors to go with your style, then you have the green light to move forward to the elements that will make that style and those colors come to life. It's the blank-canvas theory—if your room is a clean slate, a blank canvas, you are now charged with the task of painting it into a masterpiece, with each of your wedding decor elements (flowers, candles, structures, lighting, fabric draping) acting as different art mediums.

Tutera Tip: Find out about time constraints for installations for your venue so you know what you can realistically install before you budget for it. Can you imagine installing an expensive decor setup with only one hour to do it in? (Okay, so hopefully it's not that extreme, but the point still stands: Make sure your venue will allow you the time to do all you plan—and pay—for with your decor.)

STOP AND SMELL THE ROSES: FLORAL DECOR

What bride wouldn't love a free pass to buy flowers en masse? (Well, actually, I know there are some who have different preferences and may not use/want flowers at all!) Whether you feel as if you are about to spoil yourself with the aromas and beauty of your own personal, perfect garden, or are using the flowers just to strengthen your design concept, flowers make a powerful and beautiful statement.

Tutera Tip: Find flowers that are in season that are cost-effective. There are great flowers to use all year around, and my chart at the end of this chapter will help you discover what will work for you and when.

Personal Flowers—and *the* Bouquet

Personal flowers are the most important of your floral purchases, and they should be viewed as a much-needed accessory! The bridal and bridesmaid bouquets are the perfect final touch to the wedding-day fashion of your gown, your veil, and the attire of your wedding party.

The tradition of the bridal bouquet dates back to medieval times, when brides would carry clusters of herbs that were said to ward off evil spirits for protection on their wedding day. Imagine carrying garlic and other odorous stems instead of the pretty flowers that the tradition has evolved into! (Thank goodness we've come so far!) I am sure that all the brides who came before us would be happy to know your options are far less limited (and far better smelling) these days. The bouquet has now come to symbolize new life, beauty, and purity.

As the bride, you are not bound to carrying a traditional all-white bouquet; don't be afraid to be fashion-forward with your floral accessory—bridal bouquets can be colorful, trendy, creative, and fun! It used to be that if the bride wore white, the bouquet had to be white, but that is no longer the case. Personal style has introduced more and more interesting selections of color and theme into the wedding flowers, especially when it comes to the bride's bouquet.

That said, the bridal bouquet says a lot to me about a bride and how she envisions her wedding! A bouquet of white stephanotis indicates that she is classic . . . very Audrey Hepburn, timeless and beautiful. A bride who carries dripping orchids is making a dramatic statement, the fabulous center of attention! (I once had a bride who couldn't have *enough* of them! Talk about the drama!) A gorgeous bouquet of out-of-the-ordinary flowers, like anemones and cosmos and other unique blooms, reveals to me a bride who is avant-garde, daring, different, and fun. Your bridal bouquet will send a message that says a lot about you in a small—but poignant—way.

Tutera Tip: Do great things with your bouquets! They can be simple, with just florals, or you can add and embellish through many different accents. Add beading, crystals, ribbons, or pearls. . . . Incorporate a personal touch with heirlooms, like your grandmother's rosary beads or jewelry or fabrics from your ancestors. How touching would it be to carry a re-creation of your mother's or grandmother's same wedding bouquet? Colors and flowers can be manipulated wherever you can to make your bouquet special to you. Also, your bouquet can become your own with the handle: Wrapping the stems is important and also the perfect opportunity for pizzazz. Add buckles, fabric, ribbon, or faux diamonds, or specifically give it the look of your gown.

The shape of a bouquet can range from full and round to long and narrow. The round hand-tied bouquet is the most popular, but cascading bouquets are not far behind. The teardrop shape is a combination of the two, and is less formal. There is also the "cradle" style, in which the bride carries her flowers in the crook of her arm; however, this tends to be awkward—unless you're Miss America!

For bridal bouquets (and bridesmaid and junior bridesmaid bouquets), have the flower designer create each proportional to the body size of the carrier. If you are a tiny bride, you should not be carrying a full-size bouquet; it will look too large in photos and will take all the attention away from you in your dress . . . not to mention it will be excruciatingly heavy and will make your wrists sore. (Yes, really! And no bride or bridesmaid shall be swallowed by flowers on my watch.)

Tutera Tip: Flowers should never own the carrier's dress or steal the complete spotlight. (I mean, it's possible that a gorgeous necklace could stop traffic and a drop-dead gorgeous bridal bouquet could do the same at a wedding, but the point is that florals should be more like great jewelry to your dress!)

Here Come the Bridesmaids: Bouquets

Just as the style and color of your bridesmaid dresses are chosen after your bridal gown and are considered an extension to the bride, the bridesmaid bouquets should be chosen in the same sequence—after the bridal bouquet has been designed, and modeled as an extension to the bride. Once you have decided on the bridal bouquet (and the bridesmaid dress color—very crucial to this stage; you can't do your bridesmaid flowers until you have your dresses!), your bridesmaid bouquets are an easy next step.

Bridesmaid bouquets should not match your bouquet exactly, but should complement it. The bride's bouquet should always be larger and have a quality that distinguishes it, such as a slightly different flower or different colors.

Your bridesmaid bouquets are also a place where you can have some fun and take creative license! I love to meet or learn about each bridesmaid, and create matching but special bouquets for each of them that represent their individual personalities. They can also all take the same form, for a beautiful repetitious look, or can be created to be carried in interesting ways: I once made "handbags" full of florals (now there's an accessory to fashion!) and each bridesmaid carried her own design down the aisle. Add sparkles, pearls, faux diamonds, or colored stones to match the bridesmaid dress color to the inside of their (and your) blooms. Choose colors that are variations of a color palette, like blush, soft pink, mauve, and hot pink.

Tutera Tip: For a beach wedding, use conch shells full of blossoms for the bridesmaids to carry—they would make for fantastic beach bouquets.

Tutera Tip: Use leftover fabric from your bridesmaid dresses to wrap the handles of your bridesmaids' bouquets for a costless perfect match. Find some fun decoration, like crystals, beading, or something you discover at a local craft store and trim the handles. Pick something whimsical for the handle of the flower girl's bouquet!

Tutera Tip: Make custom couture roses for your bouquets by inserting petals of one rose in between petals of another rose. Mix colors and match your bridesmaid dresses in this unique way. An orchid head inside a calla lily throat is another combination for a unique twist on flowers.

The Men of Honor: Groomsmen Florals

Boutonnieres are very simple, and that's how they should stay: simple! (After all, they are for guys!) The stems that are chosen for the lapel should be an extraction of one (or a few) of the flowers in the bridal/bridesmaid bouquets. When pinning on a boutonniere, it goes on the left-hand side, just as if you were placing your hand over your heart. Two pins come with each boutonniere to secure it in place.

Don't hesitate to use a colored flower for your groomsmen's boutonnieres. Without compromising masculinity, matching blooms add style and sharp coordination.

Tutera Tip: Order two boutonnieres for your groom: one as a replacement if the first wilts. Boutonnieres have a shorter life span than your bouquet, and also, as he hugs guests, boutonnieres will tend to get crushed. With an extra on hand, he won't have the dilemma of wearing wilted flowers in your photographs.

Who Gets What?

Flowers are used to note special people in the wedding, as well as close family members and friends who hold a special place in your life. The guide below will help you order for the right people and can be adapted to your own very important guests:

- Bride—Bridal bouquet and toss bouquet
- Bridesmaids—Bouquets (a special bouquet for the maid/ matron of honor is optional)

- Junior Bridesmaids—Smaller version of the bridesmaids bouquets
- Flower Girl—Basket of petals and optionally a head wreath
- Best Man—Boutonniere
- Groomsmen—Boutonnieres
- Junior Groomsmen—Boutonnieres
- Ring Bearer—Mini-boutonniere and ring pillow
- Readers or Speakers—Corsages or boutonnieres
- Special Extended Family—Boutonnieres or corsages. This is a great way to acknowledge those who are extremely important to you (aunts, uncles, godparents, and other guests of honor) who aren't in your processional.
- Mothers and Grandmothers—Corsages or small nosegays
- Fathers and Grandfathers—Boutonnieres

DECOR THE HALLS

Ceremony Decor

My main philosophy on ceremony decor is that you *don't* have to overdecorate here. The ceremony is about love more than anything else. Your service is the real reason people are at your wedding, and all the focus should be on the bride and groom and not necessarily what the ceremony room looks like. If you don't have the budget (and even if you do), you don't have to spend a ton on flowers. Well, I'm not telling you *not* to—everyone knows I love a good over-the-top florally extravagant ceremony and I can never have enough flowers! But when you're getting down to the brass tacks of your ceremony and finding that you need to strictly and smartly spend your money, think about what's important and what's not, and spend sparingly here. Your first priority is showing the love you have for your groom to your guests who are there to witness it. Your second priority is making the room look good (not vice versa), especially when, in reality, you will be moving from that space to another in a short amount of time!

Decorating your ceremony can be broken into just a few simple areas of focus. The areas of visual design you should give attention to are:

Ceremony Area

Decorate the focal point and surroundings of where you and your groom will be standing. The ceremony structure can be a great visual for any wedding. If you need to, decorate any overhead structures above you, like chuppahs, archways, or arbors. Play up both sides of where you will be standing with floral urns of flowers on pedestals, or candelabras with or without flowers.

Tutera Tip: Your ceremony decor doesn't have to match your reception party, but it can hint at it.

Chuppahs, canopies, and archways can all be beautiful focal points that can symbolize religious or secular meaning. A chuppah (which translates to "canopy or covering") is made of a fabric supported over four poles, symbolizing the home the couple will build together. Traditionally used in Jewish weddings, the chuppah can be ornately decorated with fabrics, flowers, and even hanging candles. In Indian weddings, the ceremony takes place underneath a canopy called a *mandap*, typically elaborate and colorful with printed linings, floating drapery, and metal lanterns. If you choose to have a canopy, have your designer plan a floral design around where you and your groom will stand. Flowers above and around you create a sense of intimacy for you and your groom, and lightweight, sheer fabrics like chiffon or organza create a visual frame around you as well.

Aisle Runner

Decorating your ceremony's aisle runner is next. A simple, traditional white runner down the center of the aisle is more than sufficient, but feel free to elaborate upon it as you see fit! Add a monogram, order a custom runner with a design or your logo, or utilize colors other than white. There is no "right" way that aisle runners need to look.

Tutera Tip: *Don't forget to secure your aisle runner! Also, rope it off (with a floral garland, a ribbon, or tasteful rope) to keep guests from walking over it and messing it up with dirt, shoe prints, and wrinkles. The first steps on the aisle after it is so neatly placed down should be those of the bridal party.*

Aisle Treatment

Different than the aisle runner, the treatment is the decor that frames your aisle. As simple as dropping petals down either side of the runner, or as complex as abundant beautiful tall candle stands, aisle treatments contribute greatly to the overall look of your ceremony space. Topiaries, candelabras, floral nosegays, magnificent ribbons, floral archways, and shrubbery are all great (and fairly easy) ways to make your aisle a beautiful walkway to lead you to meet your groom.

Tutera Tip: *If your ceremony is taking place in a church, there are now a lot of regulations for decor regarding all things from ceiling suspensions to open flames on candles. Find out what you can and cannot do before you get excited about what you want with your floral designer!*

Statement Pieces

Last, decorate any other statement pieces in your ceremony space, like an arch at the beginning of your aisle where you enter. Use correlating floral, fabrics, or ribbon—you may not even need specific decor if you can just tie in these pieces with the same materials used on your larger design elements.

Use candles, candles, candles! You cannot lose with candles, across the board. Lots of candles always make a great (and inexpensive) statement and lend a very romantic, classic ambience. But please! Make sure the venue allows open flame. There are different requirements for every venue and city. Don't wait until the day of your wedding to find out that your venue will not allow your design to be installed.

YOUR DEFINING MOMENT: A CANDLE GLOSSARY

Tea Lights. Small candles used for temporary burn, approximately one-half inch in height and one and one-half inches in diameter. Tea lights are encased in thin metal, intended to be placed into decorative votive holders. Tea lights are inexpensive, with a burn life of approximately four to five hours.

Votive. Small candles approximately two inches in height and two inches in width. Also designed to fit in decorative votive holders, votive candles are used to bring an added level of light to tables and decor.

Pillar. Cylindrical and thick in shape, these candles vary in size from three to twelve inches in height, with a minimum of three inches in diameter.

Taper. Tall and narrow candles that range from six to twenty-four inches high. Used mostly in candelabras and in candlesticks, tapers project the most formal look. Taper candles are available in long and extra-long lengths.

Battery-Operated/LED Candles. Fake candles that are useful if you have restrictions on having open flames, are outdoors and facing winds, or if your designs are potentially flammable. These are a great option if you are concerned about the longevity of candle life, whereas candles that are "longer-life" also may come in handy as well.

Floating Candles. Tea lights in floating vessels or candles designed specifically to be buoyant in water. These are elegant additions to your decor. Float flowers with the candles for a simple, chic, and cost-effective decor element.

Lutera Tip: Placing votives on top or in front of mirrors creates a shimmering warm effect that gives you twice the light in the reflection.

Twice Is Nice!: Repurposing Ceremony Decor for the Reception

If your ceremony takes place in the same location in which your party is held, you may be able to reuse the decorations from the ceremony for your party. The aisle treatments can go around the perimeter of your reception room. A canopy, chuppah, or any overhead decor might be able to be relocated to go over your sweetheart table or over your fabulous cake. See what can be used again as this is a great money saver, but make sure you have a vendor (likely your florist or venue staff) that will provide the manpower and the skill to move everything from the ceremony to the dinner space. There is one small caveat: They must complete the turnover in sixty minutes (the length of time of your cocktail party). If it's possible and not chaotically suspenseful for you as a bride, it's double the pleasure.

Cocktail Hour Decor

While cocktail decor can be very minimal and just show some continuity as your guests move from one space to another, it can also have a secondary purpose of introducing the overall look of the reception party your guests are about to see through color, flowers, and style. The main decor needs for this segue party segment are as follows:

Escort Card Arrangement. Create your escort card table with height to draw attention and make a stronger introduction statement. A vase with tall flowers and lots of candles will do the trick. The linen on this table should introduce the look, but not be the same as the linens in the dining room your guests have yet to see. Lots of candles are also a wonderful addition. Leave enough room on the table for all the escort cards to be displayed.

Simple Cocktail Table Centerpieces. Both regular low tables to sit at and tall tables for people to rest drinks upon are just as simple in decor requirements as their purpose. I usually do a small bowl arrangement in the center of the table surrounded with votive candles or petals. The linen on these tables can either be a hint of what's to come in the dinner party, or an entirely different look.

Bar and Bathroom Flowers. If you have any extra money, consider doing something with fragrant flowers in restrooms or on the bar. In restrooms, use lots of candles and personalize paper hand towels with your monogram for an extra-special touch. On bars, one or two tall vertical flowers are all that are needed since people will lean on the bar while waiting for drinks and the bartender will need working space.

I DO's for Cocktail Hour Decor

- If you can't decide on just one color for the decor of your party, select two complementary colors and create alternating monochromatic table settings throughout the room for a bold and dramatic effect.
- Your cocktail hour is an opportunity to stay on a budget. Put out candles and rose petals, or clear glass bowls of water with floating flowers. That's all you need to do!
- Jazz up plain votive-candle holders. Wrap them with galax leaves or dress them with ribbons. If you're feeling particularly artsy, brush each one with a copper shade of glass paint and dip its rim in dried herbs and spices, like mint, paprika, and turmeric. By the time they dry, you will have unique and fragrant accents for the table.
- Use citrus fruit as a refreshing, inexpensive decorative element. Fill glass bowls in a variety of sizes with limes, lemons, and oranges to fill a room with color!

I DON'Ts for Cocktail Hour Decor

- Don't use scented candles at tables where food is nearby; the perfume can overwhelm guests with aromas.

- If you are outdoors in extreme heat or in a very dry indoor space, avoid using certain flowers. Ask your florist what flowers you should not use (for example, hydrangea, peonies, and sweet peas don't do well in high temperatures).

- You don't have to spend a lot of money on your cocktail hour as it's such a short time. (I'm warning you, if you spend a lot on your sixty-minute cocktail hour, you're wasting your money!) In the interim before dinner, people at cocktail hours sip a glass or two of wine, have an abbreviated bite of food, do some minimal mingling, and talk about how pretty you were in your dress. Honestly, people won't remember it, not even your pickiest relative. Use the money toward wowing everyone when they enter the room they will spend the most time in all night!

Reception Decor

At this point, you're well on your way to a well-received reception! The wedding is over, you're officially married, and the wine is a-flowing! Sounds like the perfect time to celebrate, throw a party, and really show your guests a good time!

In a job interview, they say you have seven seconds to impress your potential employer; but to wow a guest at a party, you have less than even half that to capture them and take them on a journey. Three seconds: That's all it takes to blow your guests away with a reception they will not be able to wait to partake in. Whether you're spending one dollar or one hundred dollars, this is the "gasp" moment when you have to hit out of the park. Plus, this is where your personality and your "extraordinary" dream that we talked about earlier comes alive.

Tutera Tip: *A blank party space, such as a photographer's loft, allows for any decorating option imaginable, but it's not always best for the budget-conscious. Even a minimalist approach can get costly. A great way to create a fabulous look without spending a lot is to select one or two colors and use them in abundance. One color, or one decorative item, used en masse can achieve a big WOW in any room.*

Now that we've gotten all excited, take yourself out of your perfect reverie of what you imagine your wedding will be like, because it's time to get down to the fundamentals to start concretely building that very vision.

So, you're in a blank space. Whether that's a tent, a ballroom, a reception hall, your parent's backyard, your church's social room, or the inside of a museum, here is your step-by-step guide on how to get the "WOW" effect at your reception.

Tables

Start with the internal structure of the space, which is your hard elements, like your tables. Your guests will be sitting through a dinner and for a few hours will call their seat at their table their home—this is where they will spend the most time and where most of their memories will come from. So have your guests sitting pretty! Start through shape.

All Round Tables. Most venues will have all the tables you need to make this classic and traditional look, but it may lead you down the path of the "cookie-cutter" wedding that looks just like every other wedding folks have been to. If you stick with all round tables, bring in other bold elements, whether it is varying centerpieces or some great decor options to change up your wedding and make it unique.

Long and Round Tables. This combination is perfect for making your reception more eclectic without being too out-of-the-box. When using two table shapes, there should be at least two different floral designs to match, which will make your reception visually stimulating in and of itself!

Double-Long Tables. Regal and over-the-top, two eight-foot tables placed end to end allow people to sit and face each other as if seated at a royal banquet right out of the Middle Ages. You'll feel like the queen of the castle among this fabulously formal setting.

X-shaped Tables. My favorite concept, setting tables in an X shape, encourages table talk and an unforgettable visual impression. Place one square table with one or two double-long tables on each of its four sides to make large X's in your room (I suggest making two X's and then filling in the spaces between them with rounds and longs if needed). This is an amazing way for your guests to be surprised with what they walk into, and encourages mingling as it allows them to physically see different people in many different angles as they sit. There is a sense of community with this design that I can't get enough of.

At the end of the day, your reception room shouldn't feel like there are just tables in a room, decorated. Every guest should feel like they're sitting within a private, special dining experience for the ten or so people they are with at their table at your wedding.

As far as floral centerpieces and designs, don't have your floral team create the same thing for every table—that's boring! Do a mix of arrangements that are tall and low. Floral designers are artists in their own right and floral is their medium. Structure can be as diverse as you can dream!

There are so many things you can do to your tables to make them each look like a masterpiece—again, it's like each one is a canvas.

The standard sizes of your canvases are:

Size of the Table	How Many It Seats	Size of the Cloth
54" Round	8	104"
60" Round	8–10	120"
72" Round	10–12	132"
8' Long (Rectangle)	8–10	108" × 156"

Equation: For the size of a full-length tablecloth needed, add 60 inches to your table size.

As you "paint" your table canvas, your mediums are:

Your Table Underlay Cloth. One tablecloth linen, out of two, that will dress each table. The underlay does just that—it lies underneath everything on your table, the first linen that is placed on the bottom. Your underlay will be the base color that is used to bring out an accent color of your party.

Overlay Cloth. The linen that goes on top—oftentimes, it is what we'd call the "pretty" one of the two! Overlays are either 84 inches or 90 inches. They add texture, beading, multiple colors, or print. They draw out the statement of color that illustrates your "wedding story."

Tutera Tip: See if your venue can provide in-house full-length cloths. If you are using in-house linens, make sure they are full length all the way to the floor. A table with too-short linen is like a bride with a too-short dress hem!

Chairs

Decide what color and style chairs you will use as well as how they will be decorated and dressed. Seat cushions and chair accessories like chair covers seem like just additions, but they are actually great contributors to your overall room look.

Your guest seating options will most likely include plastic folding chairs, white wood folding chairs, or the venue's existing upholstered chairs. If you choose to upgrade your seating, you will likely be renting Chiavari chairs, or ballroom chairs. The highest tier of chair rental would be custom chairs, which can be selected through rental companies based upon what styles they offer, but a high price comes along with such high style! I personally use Chiavari chairs often and think they are a great way to enhance the look of your room.

YOUR DEFINING MOMENT: A CHAIR GLOSSARY

Chiavari. A commonly found elegant chair style that originated in Chiavari, Italy. All Chiavari chairs are made to share the look of being crafted by carved bamboo joints. With a detailed back, these no-arm chairs are made of wood, resin, or metal and are available in a wide variety of colors. A cushion is required (a great opportunity to match your linens). These chairs may be used with or without coverings.

Chair Cap. A fabric covering that fits the top of the back of your chair, leaving the rest exposed. Chair caps are most often used for Chiavari chairs as they are aesthetic enough to leave parts exposed.

Chair Back. A covering that goes over the entire back of your chair, down to the floor, but leaves the seat exposed.

Chair Cover. Fabric that is custom fit to drape over the entire chair to the floor.

Tutera Tip: Never cover your chairs in spandex fabric! Spandex should never be seen at anyone's wedding (or worn, for that matter. Yikes!).

Place Setting

Setting your table with the utensils and flatware your guests will use to enjoy your bridal dinner is just as much part of the decor as the linens and the centerpieces. The china, flatware, and stemware complete the look of your design, and carefully selecting your pieces can truly bring your design home. The basic items in a place setting are:

Charger Plate. A charger plate serves as a large decorative plate to add texture and color to each place setting. It sits underneath a dinner plate and a salad plate, and is removed after the first course and entrée is eaten.

Glassware. Wineglasses, champagne flutes, and water goblets are necessary, so why not make them an intrinsic part of your design? The stem, glass, design, and accent on your glassware can all be customized. For water, wine, or both, choosing a drinking goblet in a fun design and hue adds a splash of color and presence to your table.

Flatware. Your serving utensils also serve to provide metallic accent. They can have colored handles, or bring out a glimmer of silver, gold, or bronze.

China. Dinner plates, appetizer plates, soup bowls, salad and bread plates, dessert plates, and coffee mugs and saucers fall under your china rentals. Stay consistent in pattern or deliberately mix and match designs for added interest to your table.

Room Decor

The perimeters and the rest of the room allot for the remaining room decor, if it is in your budget or overall plan. Decor for the ceiling and the four corners of your dance floor are where to focus your expenditures. Wall drapings, custom furniture, and custom cloth accents are all fantastic additions (but also very expensive). This category is last for a reason—it's decor that would be ideal to do if you have the budget, but it takes a backseat to the rest. These decor elements are great to bring into a too-large space to make a cavernous room feel intimate. They are also ideal for creating focal points within the room as well.

Dance floors: If your venue is outdoors, carpeted, or in need of a visual uplift, you may want to bring in a dance floor. Some venues have these (hotels and reception halls for certain), but if yours lacks one, you may need to go through a party rental company. Dance-floor styles can primarily be categorized as parquet (wooden pieces arranged in a mosaic or pattern), black and white (alternating black and white squares like a checkerboard), all white, or customized (with a graphic, monogram, or special design laid out onto a blank dance floor that can be easily removed), adding a great detailed look to "your" wedding!

It's standard to have about three square feet per person dancing to determine how large your dance floor should be. You know best how dance-friendly your group of guests is, but I find that about 40 to 45 percent of the guests are on the dance floor, interchangeably, at all times.

Total Number of Guests	Total Number of Dancers You Can Expect	Size of Dance Floor
60	20	10'×10'
100	30	12'×12'
150	50	15'×15'
200	70	18'×18'
275	90	20'×20'
400	140	25'×25'
600	200	30'×30'
1,000	350	40'×40'
1,500	550	50'×50'

Tutera Tip: *When in doubt of dance-floor size, err on the smaller side. A crowded dance floor is much better than a dance floor that is too large and seems unoccupied by partiers!*

I DO's for Reception Decor

- For a whimsical and romantic candlelight design, make sure you have candles in a variety of sizes and shapes—from low votives to pillar candles to tall tapered candles on candelabras—and be sure to have extras on hand in case they burn down too quickly. Setting up candles to provide different levels of light is an easy way to give your design dimension.

- Use bold, vibrant colors in your flowers and a monochromatic approach to the design to give the impression that you spent more money on the arrangements—the contrast and impact will be more dramatic and visually appealing. Also, color blocking (having individual colors clustered throughout an arrangement) is a beautiful way to incorporate several colors into your table floral designs.

- Combine florals with fruit or vegetables for a fresh and vibrant look! Grapes, asparagus, pomegranates, lemons, apples, and pears work best. Cluster the produce for a bolder statement.

- Trust your instincts: If you feel like your table is missing something, it probably is. Try adding small details, like rose petals, strands of ribbon, or small pieces of faux jewelry, such as rhinestones or pearls, to the table.

- Add something special to the napkins, as the guests are sure to notice when each picks one up to dine. I like to place single orchid heads, rose heads, mini calla lilies, or a succession of button mums on each folded napkin. Napkin rings or ribbon ties are a good final touch as well, or create sparkling napkins by adding iron-on crystals to the edges of each one. These iron-ons can be purchased at party- and sewing-supply stores.

- Go green with your centerpieces! A topiary, potted plant, or cluster of multiple styles and sizes of plants as your centerpiece not only look great but last. Have your centerpieces easily able to be taken apart so your guests can take them home and enjoy a lasting memory of the party as a favor.

I DON'Ts of Reception Decor

- When designing your table centerpieces, don't let your guests be blocked from seeing one another. When your centerpieces are in the way of the line of vision, guests can feel isolated and it will be hard for them to converse. Make sure your designer knows to either make your arrangements low, so people can see over them, or high, so people can see under them.

- Don't get trapped in thinking that your reception decor needs to match what your ceremony decor was. In fact, it's just the opposite! For one of my celebrity weddings, the ceremony was an elegant traditional ceremony, and the reception had a funky Spanish flair to it to nod toward the honeymoon location. Some of the most fun weddings are those that take guests to different places throughout the evening. They will appreciate the change in pace, and you can have two party styles in one night.

- Don't fear breaking the traditional mold of seating or reception design! Creative chairs (even mixing chair styles at different tables) or adding sofas or banquettes can be an interactive way to change things up. All you have to do then is sit back and relax in style!

MY PEOPLE WILL CALL YOUR PEOPLE: CONTACTING RENTAL VENDORS

When you rent your items (all of the above), you can either speak directly to a rental company and order these items yourself, or make your life easier and go through your wedding planner, venue, or caterer to coordinate all the logistics for getting what you need. I highly suggest having your caterer or venue serve as the go-between so you don't have to deal with shipments, returns, quantities, or anything more than simply picking out what you like.

I heard a horror story about a wedding at a church on Park Avenue, where the planner became quite concerned when her floral delivery was late. Why? Because the florists had walked into another church on Park Avenue that they thought was the venue, and set up the entire ceremony (all the florals, a big altar design, and aisle treatments). They found out it was the wrong church when someone commented that it was quite a big to-do for the funeral that was taking place later that afternoon! So give the exact directions, location name, and the name of a contact person to each of your design vendors, who will have to be there ahead of you to set up.

LET THERE BE LIGHTING!

Many brides think that lighting is an over-the-top expense that isn't worth it, but please believe me when I say lighting is one of the best things you can ever do for any party anywhere, especially a wedding. Lighting is such a key element when you're throwing a party. Picture being a superstar (which I know, is so hard to imagine . . .) and you have spent all day primping. You have the perfect outfit, the most expensive hair and makeup artists making you glamorously beautiful, and you look and feel simply fab. You're going into a photo shoot for the cover of a magazine that is going to be *the* defining moment of your life . . . and they flip on fluorescent lighting. Bad dressing room in a discount bargain basement store lighting. A glow that rivals that little bulb in your refrigerator. It just doesn't do you any justice and on top of that, no one else will see all the fabulous work that went into getting you ready and beautiful.

I think you see where I'm going with this . . . this is exactly what happens when I see brides spend lots of time and energy (not to mention money) on creating and building the most beautiful of reception parties, only to say they don't need any lighting at all, and they turn on the venue's fluorescent houselights. Lighting is what makes awe-inspiring events (the Grammys, the Oscars, the White House on Christmas) so visually stunning. Sometimes lighting is more important than decor when transforming a room to look like an unbelievable new place. From drab to fab—the fastest way to get there is through a few beams of well-placed lighting. Lighting doesn't need to break the bank or even be as complicated as it seems. Hang on for a crash course that will perhaps shed some light on the subject!

Find your lighting company by asking your venue whom they recommend. Some venues already come with an in-house or preferred vendor. If this is the case, make sure that they are affordable: Sometimes you can be locked into using a specific vendor that may be overpriced. The plus side to preferred or in-house lighting vendors is that they know the space inside and out, and their expertise is usually best this way. If you must find a lighting company on your own, do your research and ask for references of actual brides who used the company before to make sure you are getting someone reliable. Do not hire a lighting company that only does concerts and has never done a wedding before: Wedding lighting is very different from show lighting.

Tell your company you have a fixed budget and ask what they can do.

In order of importance, light your:

1. Entertainment
2. Dance floor
3. Tables

If you want to go beyond that and light the perimeter of the room (the walls), the cake, and the ceremony aisle and ceremony area, yes! Go for it! Specialty lighting in abundance is a great thing. Often lighting companies will throw in some special designs (possibly even your monogram in a light projected onto your dance floor or wall). Ask and see what ye shall receive!

Lighting is a perfect way to play to the "something different every thirty minutes" rule. Lighting colors can change and create different looks for your room that are ever-shifting (and extremely interesting to guests!). Or, if your indoor wedding is taking place while the sun is setting outside, have the lighting hues inside change in real time from daytime colors to nighttime blues and purples. I love to have the lighting change as each dinner course comes out, or as each different reception event happens (cake-cutting, father/daughter dance, etc.). Lighting is meant to be played with, manipulated, and creative. Have fun!

YOUR DEFINING MOMENT: A WEDDING LIGHTING GLOSSARY

Gobo (Monogram). A metal pattern that when placed in front of a lighting instrument casts a pattern on a surface like a floor, curtain, or wall. The metal pattern can be of texture or text, like a customized monogram or phrase that says your name and wedding date. Textured gobos (like leaf patterns, geometric shapes, and so many others!) can be placed on moving lights to add special effects to your dance floor.

Rig/Lighting Trusses/Lighting Trees. Constructions that hold up lights from above, so they project down upon your guests and dancers.

Uplighting. Ground lights that project light from underneath what is being lit.

Pinspots. Individual beams (like tiny spotlights) positioned to shine directly upon a specific spot, and that can bring attention and light to each of your tables or locations where focus should be drawn. Pinspots can be soft and colored.

Washes. Unfocused, soft lights that erase shadows and give colored light to a room. I prefer washes over pinspots because entire tables and arrangements are illuminated.

Gel. Transparent colored filters that give light its hue.

Tutera Tip: Some lighting color tints flatter skin tones more than others. Pinks, ambers, and peaches are the best choices. Using these colors in a lighting scheme gives everyone a healthy, vivacious glow. (Never use green to avoid guests looking sickly!)

Small-Scale (Nonprofessional) Lighting

If hiring a lighting company is not an option for you, ask your venue if they can provide any of those effects with what lighting equipment they have in-house. If it's minimal, have them set the dimmer switches of the houselights to half light to turn down the harshness of the bright lights (full houselights are the same as the fluorescent gymnasium look!). I also love light not just for its practical uses, but as another decor medium. Never underestimate luminaries or hand-held candles in a night ceremony or reception send-off for an unforgettable touch of romance.

Decor is just as much like a jigsaw puzzle as it is an overall artistic masterpiece. It can all come together if you have all the pieces and can see the big picture. All your elements need to fit together to create the final image. With decor, take it piece by piece, and ask your vendors to help guide you through it when you need a fresh perspective. In no time you will have a completed wedding and the only thing puzzling your guests will be how you learned to turn your wedding day into such a spectacular sight!

THE SEASONAL FLORAL CHART

*= available *(in season)*

Variety	Jan	Feb	March	April	May
Alstroemeria	*	*	*	*	*
Amaranthus	*	*	*	*	
Calla Assorted (Zantedeschia)	*	*	*	*	*
Calla Green Goddess					
Celosia Cristata	*	*	*	*	
Chrysanthemum Spray	*	*	*	*	*
Chrysanthemum Disbud	*	*	*	*	*
Cornflower			*	*	*
Daffodil					
Dahlia	*				
Delphinium	*	*	*	*	*
Freesia			*	*	*
Gardenia					
Gerbera	*	*	*	*	*
Gladioli					
Hyacinth					
Hydrangea		*	*		
Iris		*	*	*	*
Kangaroo Paw	*	*		*	*
Larkspur	*	*			
Liatris	*	*	*		
Lily of the Valley					
Lilium Casablanca (Lily)	*	*	*	*	*
Lilium Stargazer (Lily)	*	*	*	*	*
Lisianthus	*	*	*	*	*

June	July	Aug	Sept	Oct	Nov	Dec
*	*	*	*	*	*	*
*				*	*	*
	*					
*	*	*	*	*	*	*
*	*	*	*	*	*	*
*	*					
*	*	*	*			
*	*			*	*	*
*	*	*	*	*		
						*
*	*	*	*	*	*	*
						*
			*			
*	*	*	*	*	*	
*	*	*	*	*	*	*
						*
				*	*	*
				*		
*					*	*
*		*	*		*	*
*	*				*	*

(continued)

* = available *(in season)*

Variety	Jan	Feb	March	April	May
Magnolia		*	*		
Orchid Cymbidium			*	*	*
Orchid Polymin (Mini Cymbidium)			*	*	*
Orchid Paphiopedilum (Slipper)					
Orchid Phaleanopsis (Moth)	*	*	*	*	*
Paperwhites	*	*			*
Peony				*	*
Poppy					
Protea King					*
Pussy Willow					
Queen Anne's Lace		*			
Ranunculus	*	*	*	*	
Rose	*	*	*	*	*
Scabiosa			*		
Snapdragon	*	*	*	*	*
Stephanotis	*				
Stock				*	*
Sunflower	*	*	*	*	*
Trachelium	*	*	*	*	*
Tuberose	*	*	*	*	*
Tulip	*	*	*	*	*
Zinnia					

June	July	Aug	Sept	Oct	Nov	Dec
	*	*	*	*		
*	*	*	*	*		
*	*	*	*	*	*	
*	*	*	*			
	*	*		*	*	*
					*	*
*					*	*
						*
*	*	*	*			
		*				
					*	*
*	*	*	*	*	*	*
	*	*	*	*	*	*
					*	*
*	*	*	*	*	*	
*	*	*	*	*	*	*
*	*	*	*	*	*	*
	*	*				
						*
	*	*	*			

Ten

EAT, DRINK, AND BE MARRIED!: FOOD AND BEVERAGE

They say "You are what you eat!," but when designing your menu and choosing your "food and beverage," it's just the opposite. What you eat should be representative of who you are!

Food and beverage is the most expensive element of your wedding (other than design), and where you will spend the largest percentage of your budget, *but* before you get sticker shock, understand there are several things you can achieve in food and beverage while you continue to tell the story of your wedding. Yes, it's true—*food* can tell a story. . . . Putting a favorite meal on the menu reveals a little more about who you are, and makes food just another avenue to tell people something about you and your groom. An ethnic dish is more than just an entrée when it's a tribute to your culture. A fun food station that involves your guests and entertains them is not just food at your cocktail party when it's also a memory-making activity. A delectable tiramisu re-created from your grandmother's recipe or an oyster bar commemorative of your first date on a pier will pull attention away from the "need to eat" imperative, and turn it toward your creative implementations of tasty tales that your guests won't forget even long after the last bite!

The background stories of food are just part of the potential of a great menu. Visually, food can be part of your decor—an ever-changing feast for the eyes (you eat with your eyes first, then your mouth!). Think of food selection as an art form. Now, a charger plate is the canvas and with each course you are painting it with food. If you approach creating your menu as though each food is a stroke of color and texture, you will make a creation that is both beautiful and interesting, and your guests will see and enjoy their meals that way. Experiment with color and color combinations! Find foods that are comforting in taste but also interesting, tasteful, and chic.

When selecting your menu, your goal is to be interesting and inventive, without overwhelming your guests' taste buds with fancy foods out of their comfort zone. Though you may be out to impress the masses with your sophisticated taste palette, your wedding reception is not the time to get really "foodie" on people—even if you are culinary connoisseurs! Remember that your audience is your guests, and that you're literally catering to their tastes (no pun intended). When "spicing" up this portion of your event, do it through look, style, and great presentation. With food, presentation is very key . . . you want it to not only taste great, but look great; in party mode, you eat with all the senses: Bon appétit!

CREATIVELY INCORPORATING FOOD AND FESTIVITY

I once did a wedding where each table was named for a different winery. The wines served at each table were from the vineyard the table was named for. This simple but thoughtful addition to the menu did more than just quench the thirst: It depicted a large part of the married couple's personalities. The bride and groom were wine enthusiasts, and on top of that, he had proposed to her in Napa Valley. Guests who did not know that now did, and were also drawn into the couple's wedding story—something about them and now about the dining experience that would never be repeated at any other wedding. What can food say about you?

Use food to share your heritage and culture with your guests and to make your menu more about you. If you and your groom have two different cultures, have different courses represent each. Taking the extra step to make your menu so much more than a menu makes your dinner so much more memorable and unique. Pair your ethnic-inspired foods with particular wines from special regions—perhaps one from the state each of you hail from, or from a winery you have been to.

Be particular about how your food is plated. It's important to do a tasting to both taste and see—the food should taste good and also look amazing. Make the first course (appetizer) and the last course (dessert) visually beautiful. These two courses in particular set the tone for the whole meal: The appetizer is the first impression and the dessert is the last. Add garnishes, splashes of colors with your side dishes, and overall visuals, from drizzled sauces to sprinkled spices not only for flavor, but for color. Need inspiration? Make your garnishes tie into the colors and designs of your party and centerpiece.

BOTTOMS UP!: COCKTAIL HOUR

The cocktail party dates back to the 1920s—Prohibition, of course, when the desire to drink became, as we know, greater than it was even before the ban of alcohol. Speakeasies (where bartenders who served the illegal libations encouraged people doing their secretive ordering to "speak easy" when doing so) created stronger, more creative cocktails to lure in both men and women, whereas before this women rarely drank (certainly not in public!) and strong alcohol was not considered fit for the upper echelon of society. A change in times, a new law to skirt, a rise in populous venues, and a new audience to intoxicate? Behold: the birth of the cocktail party and a new way to enjoy socializing.

The cocktail hour is a crucial, albeit short part of your wedding-day flow. Meant to be a time for your guests to socialize, greet one another in a less structured scenario (versus a quiet ceremony), mingle, and meet, what better way to help them break the ice than by supplying them with various conversation-starting foods and drinks? The cocktail hour is usually just that—one hour, no more— long enough to get you and your groom from the ceremony to your reception, and short enough to avoid dragging. With food stations, specialty drinks, and fun flavors and decor, the cocktail party is a great way to get your guests ready to have a night of relaxation and fun.

Tutera Tip: The general rule of thumb for passed hors d'oeuvres: Serve five hot dishes and five cold. Steer clear of skewers with dipping sauces to keep clean.

Shy away from serving something more than finger food at a cocktail hour. Be creative and even play off your favorite foods—if you have a favorite soup, serve it in shots, which are easily passed and easily consumed. A mashed-potato bar (with mashed potatoes served in martini glasses with a variety of toppings for you to pick and choose from) is unique and also easy to execute.

Other unique ideas for cocktail hours:

- Raw bars
- Sushi bars
- Stir-fry stations
- Pasta stations
- Culturally infused food stations: Spanish/Mexican specialties, Pacific Rim, Hawaiian, Asian fusion, and so on

Have creative food stations if you have the budget! (If you do decide to have stations, know that they work just as you would expect: more stations, more money.) When speaking to your caterer, give them your guest count: If instead of "cost per station" with a lot of stations you do "cost per person," it will dictate how many food stations you will have. Then, based on your guest numbers, your caterer will present options to you. . . . Raw bar? Sushi station? Carving station? The choices can be endless. With your budget and guest count, your caterer can propose options to you as a start. See if it seems like enough food and drink to you, and either add or subtract from there. In your contract, always negotiate a guest count on the lower side—you can always add, but you can't always take away if your count turns out to be lower! Look at your timeline from start to finish, and the cost of overtime when it comes to all parts of your wedding—including your cocktail hour. If your contract says that regardless of when you start, your cocktail hour must finish by a certain time (or face overtime charges), then be sensitive to your timing to avoid paying more than you need to.

I DO's for Cocktail Hours

- Have a specialty cocktail, a specific mixed drink, cleverly named after yourselves, the place you met, or another meaningful moniker (you could even have two: one for the groom and one for the bride!). Put the name and definition at the bar. In addition to serving it from the bar, waiters should pass trays of your specialty drinks and be equipped with the drink's explanation.
- Ask for some of your favorite labels of alcohol, like a favorite scotch, tequila, or vodka (but find out what the up charge might be first!).
- Have your bars positioned farthest from the entryway. This helps the flow of guests and avoids bottle-necking at the door.

- Relax on the formality when selecting the passed foods. Fun food, even at a black-tie affair, lightens the tone. Mix in hors d'oeuvres like mini-sliders, small grilled paninis, mini-BLTs, onion soup, dumplings, risotto balls, and good ole pigs in a blanket.

I DON'Ts for Cocktail Hours

- Don't think you need to have a lot of food in order to have a great cocktail hour. An abundance of food does not necessarily make a successful wedding, especially in the cocktail hour. Food in the interim is more of a hospitable gesture, and not a meal supplement.
- You don't need to go overboard with the alcohol if you are on a tight budget! You *can* have a cost-efficient full bar. A venue's house wine and house champagne is just fine and does not need to be upgraded (and people do not typically look at the labels). If you're not on a budget, go ahead and ask for top-shelf liquor, but based on what your budget is, stay within the amount of money you have to spend without feeling pressured to increase the budget here—it's not necessary.
- Don't forget to include nonalcoholic options.
- Having a cash bar is a big *no*. It's a no for the same reason you wouldn't have a potluck dinner for your wedding: You have guests you should be treating to a night out of celebration, not work and costliness.

Tutera Tip: If you find yourself losing your appetite over food finances, don't panic! If you want to invite the people you care about and can't afford to do it the right way, think of how you can *do it the right way—there is* always *another way.* If you are in a bind with affording a big wedding, do just a cocktail party reception. If you have to choose between doing something big on a sparse budget or doing something small with a grander

budget, choose the latter—you and your guests will both enjoy
it more, and it could be more unique and memorable!

* Don't spoil the surprises! When your guests walk in to the party, everything that will be served throughout the entire party should not already be out. Have your caterers reveal different food and drinks in stages (even if you have stations, they should open up in time increments). Every thirty minutes, different foods and specialty drinks should change. This change and method of "surprise" ensures the party has a life and doesn't spoil all the fun in the first hour! All parties have to crescendo, and this is a great way to make that happen.

Having a Cocktail Party Reception

If you are throwing a cocktail party reception postceremony, make sure you indicate on your invitation, "Cocktail Reception to Follow" and request that your guests wear cocktail attire. Cocktail celebrations usually last for two to three hours. In your reception space, have at least two stationary bars as well as waitstaff serving and busing drinks, and always serve food with alcohol. When you are having a cocktail party as your main party, I suggest having a good amount of passed foods (your caterer will understand this as "heavy passed hors d'oeuvres") and/or three or four open stations that continually change foods every thirty minutes. Have dessert to follow (even by passing mini sweet treats) after you cut your wedding cake, and end your evening with drinks and dancing.

DINNER IS SERVED: DINNER RECEPTIONS

Why all the pomp and circumstance of an elaborate meal for your wedding day? Well, we can thank our medieval royals for that—

abundance of food was a sign of regality in the Middle Ages and the Renaissance period. Before the French Revolution, Marie Antoinette, infamous for wild and lavish spending on, well, everything, became known historically for the line "Let them eat cake!" in reference to her vast feasts in comparison to the peasants' meager rations. Compared to what the people commonly ate, royal feasts were extraordinary, the massive amounts of food translating to majesty and opulence. In England, King Henry VIII inherited such a large sum of money and used most of it to maintain his household—including a culinary staff of two hundred members, who provided meals of up to fourteen courses for the six hundred to eight hundred people in the king's court. Rich food, overeating, and three-hour meals became synonymous with his dynasty (and his robust figure!). It was only rich nobility that could afford such luxury, and thus, on our wedding days where our brides and grooms become royalty for the day, extravagant meals, banquets, and dinner "feast" receptions are created to be fit for the matrimonial king and queen of modern day.

The royals knew how to eat, but more so, they knew how to *dine* and be served. As the head of your reception tables, you have several options to choose from when it comes to how your meal is served! For your quick reference, the six basic styles are laid out below.

YOUR DEFINING MOMENT: A FOOD-SERVICE STYLE GLOSSARY

Buffet. Buffet style is marked by food being placed out on several large tables, and each guest table is dismissed to allow people to serve themselves. Buffet is a very common, but less formal style of food service for large events. If doing a buffet, I recommend doing as formal a buffet as possible, or keeping it to the food stations and cocktail hour. (I personally believe buffets for a wedding, even if it's not black tie, are too casual.) Buffets are often mistaken as being a large money saver (as opposed to plated meals) but beware! Buffets can actually be *more* expensive due to wasted food. Caterers cannot accurately formulate how much food needs to be made (as people always gravitate toward different dishes or vary how much food they take, so it is relatively unpredictable, causing caterers to make more food than they would for a plated dinner). If you opt for a buffet, try to budget to have the first course served plated, then the entrée and dessert courses served buffet style.

Family Style. Each table of guests is served a large portion of each course, and then encouraged to pass around to share (exactly the way a family at home would eat dinner together). This is a good option for those looking for a less-intensive service style that is more service-oriented than a buffet.

Regular Service/Plated Meals. A more formal option, each individual plate already has the food prepared on it in the kitchen, and all plates are brought out ready to serve to each table.

French Service. Food is plated at your table, prepared by tableside waiters who are serving from a larger tray of food. This is considered very elegant, but is also time consuming and so pricey. (It also has the off chance that it can go wrong . . . to me, it's almost a scientific party law that a waiter holding a piece of beef au jus over your shoulder is bound to drip it somewhere, sometime!) If you choose to have French service, make sure your waitstaff can execute it with style and grace.

Russian Service. Food is precarved into serving sizes, then reassembled to appear whole. (For example, a whole fish or a piece of roast beef would be carved in the kitchen but presented as if it had not been carved yet.) It is then brought out to your table and each serving is plated for each individual guest. The nature of this method is to be formal, but save time.

Ballet Service. Ballet service (yes, derived from the famous *Will & Grace* TV episode where, in a fit of hilarity, Jack teaches Will how to serve) is beautiful, but also quite expensive. With several waiters for each table, waiters serve simultaneously as if "performing" the service: At the same time, they sweep into the room with courses, and concurrently execute every motion together for a truly formal and special service of your wedding meal.

A TASTE OF THINGS TO COME: MENU PLANNING AND TASTINGS

With every hiring of a caterer comes a tasting: a meeting of the minds and the taste buds during which you assemble to sample a wide variety of what your caterer offers. With as few as two people (you and your groom) to as many as the two of you plus your parents, some trusted advisers from your bridal party, and your wedding planner, tastings are for you to decide what will be on your wedding-day menu. At your tasting, you will receive small portions of the larger dishes, prepared with style and accompanying wines, side dishes, and sauces.

The purpose for you is twofold: to choose what you like and also what your guests will like. When at your tasting, try everything you are hoping to have at your wedding, but as you're doing so and falling in love with certain dishes, make sure you are also thinking about your guests, who need to feel comfortable with the food that they're eating in order to enjoy themselves (and if they enjoy themselves, you'll enjoy *yourself*! You can always go out to eat your favorite dish after the wedding or the very next day, but you can't get your guests to all like it . . . sorry to the anchovy lovers out there).

Tutera Tip: Make sure your caterer knows how many people to expect at your tasting. One time I went to a fancy tasting in a hotel, and they brought out one ravioli for nine people (and trust me, it ain't pretty when nine people are fighting over one ravioli). Make sure they are preparing enough food for everyone to actually taste at the tasting!

I DO's for Meeting with Your Caterer

* Ask how many waiters you are getting per table for service. Insist on one waiter per table. If you're having black tie, and are really looking for impeccable service, you need two waiters for really great service.

RAISING THE BAR: BARS AND WAITERS PER GUEST

Number of Guests	How Many Waiters (Casual)	How Many Waiters (Formal)	How Many Bars	How Many Bartenders?
50	5	8	1	1
100	10	15	1 or 2	2
150	15	23	2 or 3	3
200	20	30	3 or 4	4

Tutera Tip: Decide with your caterer how many bars to have. Have bars in your dining room, but also have waitstaff be able to serve your guests drinks at their tables when they start eating (to keep your guests from getting up and down during a meal). If a guest wants, say, vodka straight up with a lemon twist on the rocks, and your dinner drink service only includes wine, your waiter should be able to bring requested drinks to the table.

* Ask how the food is being serviced. Will it be brought out and put on tray jacks (please say no!), or will it be brought out with silver lids ("hats") that get removed (and are they the fancy hats . . . or the "just keep the food warm as long as you can" lids?). You want your service to be comprehensive, but as the formality of service style increases, so does the price (why does that always happen?).
* Ask your caterer about the timeline of the food service. My philosophy is that each course should be served, eaten, and cleared in thirty minutes (no matter how many people you

have in attendance) to keep the party going. Your caterer may think it important to let your guests take their time to enjoy their meal (as expected, a good caterer should value food as the most important thing!) but to me a good wedding is gauged by how much fun people are having. Slow dining and service also directly stall the pace of the entire wedding flow.

- Do ask your caterer beforehand to cook to their strongest suits! Ask them to prepare some of your requested dishes, but also to surprise you with a few of their specialties. You never know what they have cooking, and you won't know what you're missing out on unless you try.

- Do have a great time at your tasting! Enjoy the moment of sitting down and dining. (What a great task—to eat!)

I DON'Ts of Meeting with Your Caterer

- Don't forget to look at the presentation of the food. In addition to evaluating the taste of the food, you are meeting with your caterer to consider the look and the placement of your food. Especially with drizzled sauces, creatively stacked dishes (i.e., filet on top of mashed potatoes or rice pilaf, topped with a garnish), and combinations of multiple colors and sizes of foods (like vegetable medleys), pay attention to the display. If a dish looks sloppy rather than neatly presented, politely ask the chef to "tighten up" the plate for show.

- Don't get frustrated if people at your tasting disagree with one another. (Aunt Jo might be adamant that the beef is too dry when your mother-in-law thinks it's just fine!) There's sense to the phrase "There are too many cooks in the kitchen!" At the end of the day, make sure *you* are making the final decisions, to the best of your ability. If there is heated chatter about whose tastes are more refined, table the discussion and discuss that particular dish with the chef later, without your entourage.

- Don't get carried away! Know what should be on a traditional seated dinner menu, and keep it that way. A traditional menu is three parts: appetizer, entrée, and dessert. You don't need six courses. Some places think it's a must to have soup, a salad, intermezzos, etc., etc. . . . but your guests may not see it as a luxury (and may secretly be yelling, "Enough with the food! OK, we get it! You love food . . ."), and it's not necessary to have tons and tons of it. In fact . . . the more you feed people, the more full they feel, and the less they dance (and the more the mood of your party changes!).

Food-Friendly Unique Ideas

Mix it up. "Duets" or "trios" bring novelty to your dinner courses. Having different flavors and choices among an appetizer or entrée shakes things up! Sampling foods is fun and visual and provides the indulgence of a wider selection (but do not do it every course—that's too much!).

TRIO (BEST USED WITH APPETIZERS)
- **French fry trio** Regular, sweet potato, and polenta fries elegantly served in cones with bride and groom's monogram, with three different gourmet sauces.
- **Mac 'n' cheese trio** Traditional, jalapeño and pancetta, truffle with Parmesan

DUET (IDEAL FOR ENTRÉES)
- **Beef duo** Braised short ribs with petit filet mignon
- **Seafood duo** Encrusted halibut with grilled lobster tail

FOUR OR MORE (USE FOR FUN DESSERTS)
- Have a variety of sweet after-dinner tastes with an assortment of small dessert bites. For a bachelorette party once, I served a sampling of seven "simply sinful" sweets!

Lutera Tip: Some people may not be able to eat your menu selections due to
dietary restrictions, religious reasons, or allergies (the most
common are gluten, peanut, and MSG). In selecting your menu,
ask your caterer to have a vegetarian option on hand (a good
caterer will know how many vegetarians you might have by
percentage based upon your guest count). If you do decide to
have kids at your wedding, count your kid Rsvps so you can
plan to offer a child-friendly meal, and ask for a greatly
reduced cost per child.

PLAYING WITH YOUR FOOD: FOOD AS ENTERTAINMENT

I'm a firm believer that it is far from appropriate to play with your
food at a formal grown-up meal, but there is actually a huge excep-
tion to that rule, and it's all in the name of entertaining your wedding guests! In your roles as host and hostess, you and your groom
can easily take on the fun challenge of making every part of your
party something new or interesting to the guests, and through what
you can do with food, it is all the more possible to enthrall and
involve them at every step. (Food can also be entertainment if done
right!) Even in the most formal of settings, making your cuisine
unique and even lighthearted is not just acceptable—I highly encourage it! One of the most elaborate elegant weddings I did in a
grand ballroom included a food station with three huge silver tu-
reens filled with dry ice, manned by three chefs concocting amazing
raspberry liqueur desserts. The excitingly dramatic smoke from the
dry ice drew the attention of the guests, and the sweet treat was both
delightful and surprising. The bride said to me, "Now *there* is a
course to remember!," and I thought to myself how worthwhile it
to do something more than just serving a raspberry torte on a plate!
Another bride of mine wanted to herald her Mexican roots, and we

served a special native coffee, heated over an open flame with a special cream design drizzled into each glass: a fun and fiery treat to drink and to watch being prepared. I'll also never forget a "Limoncello" dessert bar—lemon trees with ice bases, with frozen Limoncello bottles placed among glistening rocks of ice. Shot glasses made out of ice were available for guests to partake in this sweet experience!

Go outside the lines when concocting your dream dessert. Dessert is a good place to let loose and break the formality of a wedding. Colored sorbets in your wedding colors can be a thought-provoking touch. Cotton candy, available in all colors, can bring a bridesmaid-dress-matching hue to the side of a plated dessert's dish. Find out how your dishes can be abstract or embellished through hardened chocolate, royal icing, or any sculpted sweetness.

Have an alternate dessert besides your wedding cake . . . who says you can't have your cake, and eat more dessert, too?

UNIQUE DESSERT IDEAS

Be Fun. Have cheesecake lollipops, gourmet Oreos, and shot-glass milkshakes

Be Different. Serve differently decorated mini wedding cakes to each table

Be Sweet. Have multiple sweet treats (cookies, brownies, tarts, cupcakes, and lemon bars) brought to each table on trays and passed around on the dance floor

Be Seasonal. Serve lavender sorbet in sugared baskets, decorated with white chocolate butterflies (spring); mini popsicles, ice-cream sandwiches, and chilled fruit skewers (summer); mini deep-dish apple pies (fall); or hot cocoa or chocolate shots rimmed in crushed peppermint candy with fresh hot doughnuts (winter)

Give dessert the credit it's due—it's my favorite course, and I love to make it a celebration of its own with a dessert bar. If your party is able to move in location, set up a dessert bar in an entirely new setting where guests can enjoy their last course. Go from a romantic ceremony to an elegant dinner, and then into a festive and chic dessert lounge. Change the music, the lighting, and the color scheme, and dance away as this dining finale becomes a whole new experience of your party. Have the cake-cutting in your new location as well.

The wedding cake is a traditional staple, just as much an event element as it is a dessert, but don't feel as though your only dessert choice is to have a traditional wedding cake! More and more, brides are exploring the options of having creative desserts, alternatives to the familiar white wedding cake, such as serving a wedding cake to each table or serving up treats that are more aligned with their personalities. . . . Here are some tips for finding your biggest dream dessert of all.

LET THEM EAT CAKE!: FAULTLESSLY FINDING YOUR FUTURE CONFECTION

Finding a Baker

When searching for the right baker, it's all a matter of having good *taste*! You must like both of the baker's "tastes": his or her taste in decorating with artistic style and ability, and also the "taste" of the final cake product produced with the baker's culinary skills.

To truly determine if a baker will "cut it" in both of these arenas, going in for a cake tasting is a must—meeting your baker, sampling several options, and discussing with him or her your overall vision for your one-and-only wedding cake is critical to making you feel comfortable about such a momentous part of your day. Ask for references from other brides who have already used this baker, and only hire a baker you feel you can trust.

Formulating Your Cake Design: Cake and the Style of Your Wedding

After selecting your baker, discuss in depth the design you envision for your cake. Also see what your baker may have in mind given the description of your wedding style, colors, dress, location, and flowers. Wedding cake designers are artistic professionals who use frosting as their art medium, and may have brilliant creative ideas (either to design your cake from scratch or to add on to your concept). Inquire about how your baker's cakes are made, what ingredients are used, and how he or she keeps cakes fresh.

A wedding cake can match the design of the wedding, the personality of the bride and groom, the wedding flowers, or even the pattern or style of the wedding gown. If for a destination wedding, it can even beautifully resemble the venue or location. Cake design ideas are limitless: Let go of tried-and-true designs (the old "basket weave" and other regular patterns) and let your baker become your artist and give you ideas that represent you as a couple.

Flavors

If you have trouble deciding on one cake flavor and one filling flavor to serve, let each layer be a different flavor with a different filling. Once the cake is sliced and on plates, guests can pick their favorite. Whatever you do, make sure you taste all your options (especially the one you decide you'll want for your actual cake) because you want it to taste fabulous as well as look great since all of your guests will be tasting it with you!

Fondant and Frostings

The two main frostings to choose between (while there are many out there) are fondant and buttercream frosting. Fondant is the smoother, thicker of the two (it is the "picture-perfect" frosting that has a uniform smoothness—like a hard shell of frosting—and gives the baker the ability to build and sculpt your cake and all its decorations). While it has the look of smooth perfection, it is lacking in taste.

Buttercream is purely about the quality of taste and sweetness. While it cannot be smoothed and shaped as well as fondant can, it can still be beautiful and is the best option for those who choose taste over sight. Made out of sugar, whipped eggs, and butter, a buttercream-frosted cake is the freshest cake you can get; it needs to be created and frosted within a short time frame so the frosting won't spoil.

Your taste buds will make the decision—but you will make the commitment between art . . . or taste.

Regardless of which you choose, when it comes to decorating, there isn't anything you *can't* do with sugar icing. (They say you can get lots of bees with honey, but you can get all your guests buzzing with some creatively sculpted sweetness!)

Flowers

If frosting or sugar flowers are adding up expensively, don't forget that having real flowers atop your dream cake may be more cost-efficient and just as beautiful. Coordinate with your baker and your florist to make sure that the floral prepared for your cake topping is the correct size and weight to add on. Add florals around the bottom of your cake to mask the stand or disc the cake is displayed on and to finish off your cake's look.

Fillings

The possibilities for cake fillings are almost endless, so just enjoy the tongue-tripping tastings to select your favorite! Some bakers have specialties, so ask what has been popular among their clientele. If you have certain fruits you enjoy most (I have seen a tangerine filling) or fruits from a certain region you hail from (passion fruit filling, anyone?), it doesn't hurt to ask if it can be incorporated in your cake to make it more personalized to you and your groom.

Tutera Tip: Once, for a celebrity wedding, I made the bride a beautiful white cake: white frosting, white cake, white everything. . . . The cake slices were placed at a dessert station, full of a vast array of toppings (from berries to sauces, chocolate, and more) for each guest to make their own cake to their personal taste in a fun, unique, interactive (and tasty) way!

Flawlessly Faking It: Sheet Cakes/Fake the Cake

There's no sugarcoating it: Wedding cakes are expensive! But there is a tip I've shared with some of my eager cost cutters: A wedding cake is easy to fake.

There are certain companies that are specifically in the business of making fake wedding cakes—constructions of Styrofoam crafted to appear convincingly realistic. These are then decorated just as if they are regular wedding cakes, prepped for detail and all your frosting, flower, or ribbon-trimmed requests. They leave a section for a bit of real cake to be frosted right into it, so you can actually still have a cake-cutting (as if your guests weren't fooled enough!). As with regular wedding cakes, the waitstaff wheels it away into the back to slice it—but instead they box it up, slice up a more cost-efficient sheet cake, and bring this other cake out to your guests. I have to admit, even I haven't been able to tell sometimes if a fake cake is indeed fake—the right vendor can make this your best financial move, when the only thing bigger than your secret is the amount of money you saved.

Tutera Tip: Cupcakes are also a fun twist on the traditional wedding cake—have tiers of cupcakes frosted in white or in your wedding colors delivered to each table during the dessert course. Have the cupcake baker make you and your groom a larger version of a cupcake to still have a cake-cutting of your own.

Freezing Your Cake

Ask your caterer to make sure they save the top tier of your wedding cake for your first anniversary. When you get home (or this could be a task for an eager-to-help mother-in-law?), wrap it with plastic cling wrap and then keep it in a moisture-proof vacuum-sealed freezer bag after first getting rid of as much excess air as possible. Originally, the tradition was to keep this cake for the christening party of the couple's first child, but now tradition holds that one year from your wedding date, you and your groom should unfreeze the top and eat it with a bottle of bubbly to celebrate your successful anniversary.

Final Finishing Touches

For a truly unforgettable cake-cutting, have a cake served to each table, and have them cut into their cake at the same time you cut into yours! This gets guests involved and makes the cake-cutting more fun for everyone and very memorable (and each table wishes you good luck as they cut!).

Ask your caterer to provide (or purchase yourself) small, colorful gift boxes and ribbon or twine to box up individual slices of the cake. Tie on precut notes from you, the bride and groom. This way, your guests can take home any leftover cake and have "sweet dreams" of the party.

Eleven

GET ME TO THE CHURCH ON TIME!: TIMELINES AND LOGISTICS

With all the working pieces you've planned to make your wedding day complete, it's now time to organize them in schedule form to put those plans in motion. In the wedding world, well-created and well-executed timelines and logistics make good wedding planners and good weddings. The main differences between good weddings and *great* weddings all lie hidden in the behind-the-scenes coordination. The schedule to your wedding is the script to a movie, the playbook to a winning game, the answer to the call, the key to unlock all the unanswered questions of the universe. . . . Well, maybe not all that, but in wedding terms, it is the backbone of the happiest day of your life, as well as the guide to allowing your vendors to run it for you with ease instead of stress. On the one day that your wedding is your world and everything revolves around the bride, something that important sounds like the key to the universe to me! Put all your hard work to the test and lay out your timeline to make sure that everything happens when it should happen, and that you have allotted enough time to do everything and enjoy it all as you go along.

IN DUE TIME

Begin with anchoring the main components of your day where they need to be: your ceremony, cocktail hour, and reception. Once those are in place, you can fill in the other wedding activities you need to partake in and gauge when you need to start and finish each one to begin the next.

It's important to know how long your service will last before you commit to the time of your reception. Ask your officiant for a time estimate, and if you have a lot of parts (readers, musical performers, or other components), it's a good idea to walk through it in person to get an accurate assessment of how long it will take. Write a script to really make sure you stay on track.

In its own clockwork, for all shows on Broadway, the curtain goes up at 8:07 P.M. for every performance that "starts" at 8:00 P.M. I stand true to the same tactic with your wedding! "Invite time" (the time you will put on the invitation) should always be thirty minutes before your ceremony will start. If you plan to walk down the aisle at 7:30 P.M., your invite should read 7:00 P.M. Like with any party, guests should know to arrive earlier than the invite time to give themselves ample time to settle in and find seats in time for your big reveal, but there are almost always latecomers.

DOWN TO THE MINUTE!: THREE SCHEDULE SCENARIOS

The most important rule when planning a wedding is that there are no rules or boundaries. (I know that may come as a shock, but read on.) Many of my brides and grooms come to me with the notion that they have to do certain things when making their wedding-day plans and schedules. I try to encourage ideas that go beyond the limit my clients have set in their minds. You should take every opportunity to infuse your own personal ideas into each element of the day, including the timeline of how it's run itself. The three timelines below can give you an idea of various ways to structure your wedding day—from the very traditional, to traditional with a twist, to entirely unique. They are here to serve as a guide for you to form your own wedding-day timeline and get you where you need to go the way you want to get there—with time to spare.

Scenario 1: Traditional Timeline

This traditional timeline is as stress-free as it gets! For a wedding that takes place in the same location (or nearby) as the reception, the timeline is simple and your biggest concern is just staying on schedule. For an evening ceremony followed by a dinner reception, stay traditional to your wedding and also to your timeline, as follows:

CEREMONY TIMELINE

2:00 P.M. All limos to arrive at bride's parent's home and groom's home

2:45 P.M. Groomsmen's limo leaves for church

3:00 P.M. Bridesmaids' limo and bride's limo to leave for church

3:30 P.M. Ceremony to start

4:30 P.M. Ceremony to finish

COCKTAILS AND RECEPTION TIMELINE

5:30 P.M. Guests to arrive at cocktail hour in cocktail room

6:25 P.M. Guests called to enter dining room

6:30 P.M. Dinner and dancing in main ballroom

6:40 P.M. Bridal party announced into room

Entrance of Full Bridal Party:

Bridesmaids and Groomsmen

Flower Girl and Ring Bearer

Maid/Matron of Honor and Best Man

Bride and Groom

6:50 P.M. Bride and groom go straight into first dance

Bridal party to join halfway through, along with guests

7:25 P.M. Appetizer served

Dancing until band announces special dances

Father of the bride speaks

7:30 P.M. Blessing of the food

8:00 P.M. Dance set

8:30 P.M. Band announces special dances

Father/daughter dance

Mother/son dance

8:45 P.M. Entrée served

Band announces toasts

Best man toast

Maid of honor toast

9:30 P.M. Band plays a high-energy dance music set

10:00 P.M. Wedding cake brought onto dance floor

Band to ask guests to take their seats and bridal

party to join the couple on the dance floor

Once couple takes first bite of cake, music plays and

confetti cannons go off at kiss

Dance set

10:15 P.M. Dessert served and bride does bouquet toss

10:30 P.M. Reception concludes, guests invited into after party

Midnight Two town cars to arrive for bride and groom and
parents

After party concludes for guests

Scenario 2: Progressive Wedding

One of my lucky brides had a church ceremony that was able to be
immediately followed by a hotel reception! While there is usually a
lapse of time between a ceremony that takes place in a house of
worship, and a reception (especially in a hotel), this particular bride
avoided this by planning. By not committing to a specific date and
first finding out what worked for both the church and the hotel, we
were able to make this bride and groom's wedding a seamless transi-
tion. And seamless transitions continued all night—the bride wanted
something never done before, so I found a hotel that allowed us to
close down the grand lobby for cocktails, then use two ballrooms for
dinner in one and dessert and dancing in the other. This constant
movement of guests played well thanks to a detailed timeline and
vendors who all followed closely along.

CEREMONY TIMELINE

4:30 P.M. Bridal party to depart for church/arrive at holding
room

Entire bridal party to receive personal flowers

5:30 P.M. Entire bridal party to be lined up for processional,
ready to walk down the aisle

5:45 P.M. Musician to begin playing organ as guests arrive

6:00 P.M. Ceremony begins with processional at the church

7:00 P.M. Recessional

7:15 P.M. Photos on altar with entire bridal party

COCKTAILS AND RECEPTION TIMELINE

7:30 P.M. Cocktails in the lobby of the hotel

Musical trio performs all standards and Cole Porter
piano

7:45 P.M. Musical trio plays transitional music

7:55 P.M. Music change

8:00 P.M. Bride and groom enter after trio introduces them

8:05 P.M. First dance

8:10 P.M. Father/Daughter dance

8:15 P.M. Mother/Son dance

8:20 P.M. Bridal party to dance

8:30 P.M. Trio performs for thirty more minutes

8:45 P.M. Call to dinner in first ballroom

9:00 P.M. Pianist performs throughout dinner

9:05 P.M. *Amuse-bouche* (a small appetizer) is served

9:10 P.M. Blessing

9:20 P.M. Toast by father of the bride

Amuse-bouche is cleared

9:25 P.M. First course is served

9:35 P.M. Toasts by friends of the groom

Toasts by friends of the bride

9:55 P.M. First course is cleared

10:05 P.M. Main entrée is served

10:25 P.M. Toasts by best man and maid/matron of honor

10:35 P.M. Guests asked to move to dessert lounge for dessert

and dancing in second ballroom

Bride and groom exit first, guests to follow

Bride and groom change clothes

Band performs in dessert lounge

11:00 P.M. Bride and groom make second entrance

11:25 P.M. Bride and groom perform cake-cutting ceremony

11:35 P.M. Second dance with bride and groom

11:40 P.M. Bouquet toss

Midnight Party ends

Scenario 3: Outdoor Wedding

This third scenario is the most unique timeline I have ever done. It's daring and memorable, which is what I love! It began unusually, with the bride and groom having cocktails and dinner with their guests first, followed by their nighttime ceremony. Guests were given candles and led to line an aisle for the bride and groom to walk through. At the end of this aisle, they arrived at a floating dock for their ceremony, and their guests surrounded them as they wed for a wedding no one would ever forget.

COCKTAILS AND RECEPTION TIMELINE

4:50 P.M.	Musicians begin playing for cocktail hour in garden
5:00–6:00 P.M.	Cocktail hour in garden, music plays throughout
5:00 P.M.	The reception band arrives
5:15 P.M.	Strolling musicians arrive for dinner
6:00 P.M.	Guests start to move to main tent for dinner
6:10 P.M.	First course is served
6:15 P.M.	Blessing (note: music stops)
6:20 P.M.	Maid/matron of honor makes a toast
6:25 P.M.	Musicians continue to stroll
6:30 P.M.	The strings arrive to set up at ceremony area
6:40 P.M.	First course is cleared
6:45 P.M.	Family-style main course is served to tables
6:55 P.M.	Bride and groom make toasts to each other

CEREMONY TIMELINE

7:30 P.M.	Bride and groom leave to go and change into ceremony fashion in main house
7:40 P.M.	Waiters in place with baskets of candles, to help guests into position String musicians begin to perform in forest
7:45 P.M.	Guests are requested to depart the tent and make their way to the ceremony site. They are greeted by waiters who pass out candles. Violins escort guests into the aisle area. Planning staff to turn over tent to dessert area.

8:10 P.M. Ceremony in the forest

Music starts, to indicate ceremony is going to begin

Bride enters; walks down aisle, meets groom halfway

8:20 P.M. Ceremony begins

8:30 P.M. Sunset

8:50 P.M. Ceremony is over

Fireworks

8:55 P.M. Guests make their way back to tent for dessert

9:00 P.M. Dancing and dessert in tent

9:05 P.M. Bride and groom dance their first dance

9:10 P.M. High-energy dance set

10:30 P.M. Bride cuts the cake

High-energy dance set starts immediately after cake-cutting ends

10:50 P.M. Coffee and mini-desserts come out and are passed along with the cake

11:45 P.M. Party ends

Buses return to departure destination

Tutera Tip: *No matter the time of year, look up the sunrise and sunset of your wedding day on a weather Web site or in* Farmers' Almanac *to plan accurately for lighting needs, ceremony and reception timing (if it is outdoors), and photograph-taking in the light you need. Take advantage of Mother Nature at her best!*

Tutera Tip: *A "turnover" is a party term used to describe the changing of a space that was used for one purpose into an entirely new party space while the guests are absent. The turnover in this scenario was converting the tent used for dinner into a dessert-and-dance lounge, all while the guests were at the ceremony. Tables are moved, decor is changed, sometimes even the florals, colors, and designs are all different by the time the guests return. Turnovers are exciting and fascinating for the guests, but they take manpower and organization and cannot run late!*

Tutera Tip: By now, you know how much I love to have something different happen every thirty minutes at a party, especially a wedding. As you're making a timeline, take into consideration what you will be changing after each increment of time. Some starter ideas:

- Movement of people
- Change in predictable timeline
- Music change
- Color of lights change
- Toasts
- Special dances
- Moving locations from dinner to dessert

WHEN TIME IS ON YOUR SIDE: LAPSES BETWEEN CEREMONY AND RECEPTION

It's never ideal to have a lapse of time between your wedding ceremony and your reception, so whenever possible, please avoid this scenario! Many times, though, this is par for the course when booking in a house of worship because many weekend days must be shared with other couples getting married, resulting in a designated time slot that may be hours before a dinner reception should start. In these time lapses, the party flow is not just stalled but halted, and guests are forced to occupy themselves for an odd space of time (too short to go home, too long to ignore!). You have a cushion of not more than two hours of overlapping time before your guests begin to feel uncomfortable, lost, or unsure of what to do, and worst of all, sometimes guest count can even diminish for either your ceremony or your reception. You want everyone to be there for both. If having more than two hours of time between ceremony and cocktails cannot be avoided on your particular date, I strongly recommend reconsidering your date (yes, I am that passionate about you keeping your attendance up and your guests happy!).

If you have an acceptable lapse of time, host a brunch in your home, or a small gathering for your immediate family and out-of-towners. For all your guests, have a hostess hand out a list of local activities, parks, historic sites, and sightseeing locations at the end of the ceremony to give them options to entertain themselves as they wait for your reception to begin. A great way to do this is to provide a map pinpointed with your favorite spots as a couple—a restaurant you had your first date in, the place he proposed, a park where you spent the Fourth of July, your favorite coffee shop. . . . In everything you do in your wedding, there is always a way to further tell your story, and this is also a perfect opportunity to share a part of your lives your guests may not yet know.

Tutera Tip: Ask how much time there is before and after your wedding ceremony (namely, if it's in a church), as sometimes wedding ceremonies are booked back to back with little to no time to decorate, have a receiving line, or take photos. Don't get your time slot and assume you'll have all the time to do what you are hoping to! Know for certain what is before or after your service, and then plan accordingly.

POINT A TO POINT B: TRANSPORTATION

Planes, trains, and automobiles . . . the phrase doesn't do justice to the categories that also encompass Lear jets, the Orient Express, and Porsche convertibles! Nor does "mode of transportation" begin to describe the options you have to arrive in style to your wedding. It doesn't just have to be a drop-off and pickup in a car anymore. . . . Transportation has even gone as far as the bride I had who canoed down a river to her outdoor wedding. She got to a rock point where her groom met her on a white horse. (Try adding those to the planes, trains, and automobiles list.) They said "I do" and then rode off together into the sunset. . . . Sound picturesque? Almost surreal? It's all timing and planning, and if you do it right, anything is possible for your dream entrance and exit through the right transportation.

While a large part of transportation planning is determining how you and your groom will get to and from your ceremony and reception with pizzazz, it also covers the transportation of your guests and bridal party and how they will be arriving to your wedding (not to mention what "transportation" means for a destination wedding!). Without good solid plans for transporting yourselves and your people, you won't have your guests or bridal party in the right place at the right time—and that's very important to the rest of the picture! You cannot assume you can book transportation vendors and have them show up and everything will be smooth sailing. Getting everyone from point A to point B is a potential disaster if it's not taken care of precisely, by you and by your transportation company. Especially the day of, keep close tabs on your drivers. Regardless of whether you have rented a bus, car, limo, trolley, carriage, moped, and so on, have phone numbers of the company as well as numbers for each driver on hand. Have a point person who knows who is driving and who is being driven at all times, and supply that person with a backup plan (discuss with your vendor) in case something breaks down.

Why so important? Untimely transportation is the catalyst for the flow of events and the timeline falling apart if not taken care of properly. Your wedding actually *starts* and *ends* with transportation. The moment you or your guests get into a car and mobilize toward your party, it's off and running and the wedding-day gears start turning. If a car (can you imagine if it were to be yours!) gets lost and the ceremony starts late, the timeline is off and it is impossible to make up for lost time. . . . The reception then begins late, and then the band is on overtime, and before you know it, because of one transportation hiccup, your budget could be blown.

So that may sound a bit dramatic—being late is not the end of the world—but it *is* a very serious matter and can have severe consequences (just think of Patrick Dempsey in *Made of Honor* when he missed the ferry to the Irish wedding. He ended up needing to hijack a truck and a horse because he was just a few minutes too late!). You can save yourself lots of headache and money if you plan ahead so you stay on time. The only reason you should pay extra for running late is because you're having so much fun and you insist that you just cannot stop dancing. And as good as Patrick Dempsey looked doing it, I still would like to prevent you from hijacking any kind of truck along the way.

DON'T DO THE PINK STRETCH LIMO: TRANSPORTING YOURSELF TO YOUR WEDDING

Maybe you are having a fun pier-side wedding and you can't see yourself in anything but a windblown veil trailing behind you as you speed off on a moped. Perhaps you're the quintessential princess bride that has always been destined to arrive in a white horse-drawn carriage. Maybe you've always wanted the simplicity and elitism that comes with a black stretch limousine with all the bells and whistles inside to enjoy with your bridal party. Or possibly, you are marrying in a cultural hotspot like San Francisco where arrival by trolley is almost second nature. Transportation might be a way for you to further your theme—an old Hollywood–style wedding would only be right if a vintage car brought you to it! For your exit at the end of the reception, will you reveal a surprise Ferrari to speed you away to your honeymoon? Enjoy discovering what is right for you and what will express who you are in this fun way. May your wedding transportation never be a boring logistic—it should be just as fun as the photos you will have capturing you on it, in it, or driving it away! Some transportation ideas:

- Limos
- Horse-drawn carriages
- Buses
- Party buses
- Antique cars

Tutera Tip: Make sure the air conditioner works in antique cars. You can get motion sickness very quickly when you are all dressed up, with hair done and makeup on, and then have to take a ride in a car on a hot day with no air-conditioning—not a good way to start your big day!

- Town cars
- Exotic sports cars
- Vespas and mopeds
- Rickshaws
- Hayrides
- Trolleys
- Boats
- Helicopters
- Bicycles
- Hot-air Balloons
- Motorcycles

As creative as you may get, remember to partake in your transportation with class! If your modes of transport come in a variety of colors, I say add a touch of sophistication and style by moving away from the bright pinks and oranges and choosing classic white and black. Also make sure you are able to get on and off your transportation gracefully in your wedding attire—you may have an usher standing by ready to help you.

WHICH WAY DO WE GO?:
DIRECTIONS FOR GUESTS

Having your guests there is half the party! Giving out clear directions to every location they will need to find helps them be on time (and helps you by preventing latecomers to your ceremony!). Make the drives from place to place yourself to see how long it takes you and what tips you can add to make the routes as easy as possible. Provide driving routes from all directions: north, south, east, and west, and from all major highways, airports, and train stations. Give your guests an accurate measure of how far the distance is from main points to your venues, along with an approximate length of time it will take to get there.

Avoid having your events happen anywhere near rush hour. I've seen many a guest walk in to the reception already in need of a cocktail from sitting in rush-hour traffic and feeling the stress of being late! Also do your research on what is happening in the city on your wedding date: Are any roads going to be closed? Will there be construction? If it's an area you don't live in, send someone there to check it out. Find out if festivals, parades, street closures, or concerts are occurring so you can avoid running late before you even begin.

THERE AND BACK: TRANSPORTING
YOUR BRIDAL PARTY AND/OR GUESTS

If your venue is out of the way (like up a mountain), difficult to find, or if parking is limited, it is customary to provide transportation for your guests. Arrange a meeting point, where your guests can be picked up and have enough transportation to keep guests from waiting in line for a ride. It is also ideal to provide special transportation for your bridal party, as they will be as dressed up as you will be, and it is in your best interest to keep them all together to ensure they are stress-free and that there are no stragglers! Keep the bridal party's transportation separate from the general guest transportation.

If you are providing transportation for your guests and/or bridal party, your options may be narrowed down based on guest count or bridal party numbers. For group transportation, either guest or bridal party, consider the following options based on capacity:

Mode of Transport	Passenger Capacity
Van	6 to 12
Bus	25 to 50
Town Car	2 to 4
Limousine	6 to 12
Stretch Limo (SUV, Hummer)	12 to 30
Specialty Cars (Ex: a vintage 1955 Rolls-Royce)	2 to 4
Sports Car	2

Tutera Tip: Just like sending a wedding gift, it's better for your wedding party to arrive early than late!

The worst feeling for a guest is having no way out! Even if they don't want to leave, knowing they have the option is a comfort. If you have buses bringing guests home from the venue, make sure they depart in staggered runs. You don't want your guests to feel like they're being held hostage at your venue, only to be anticipating their release by the arrival of the transportation! This may mean your transportation consists of smaller vehicles making multiple trips rather than making everyone wait to fill a fifty-passenger bus.

If you are the bride and groom, educate others so they can serve as the points of contact to guests who have questions or put all transportation information into an itinerary. You'll want to be able to be free to do your own thing, coming and going as you please (you're a bride—not a "field-trip mom"!). The point person should be the last to leave for the venue (and from the venue on the way home). Ask someone outside of your bridal party (not a maid of honor who has to be somewhere at a certain time and will have to leave everyone hanging with questions). And ask nicely! Remember, this job is a labor of love.

A note on designated driving: If you're serving lots of alcohol at your wedding, have transportation at the ready. Call taxi companies beforehand and express interest in referring them to your guests, or hire a few town cars to run from your reception to your guests' hotels in the last hour of your reception.

THE DRIVING FORCE: VALET

If you have a valet service at your wedding, remember it is the first thing guests experience at a wedding and also the last. That said, make sure the valet experience is smooth, calm, and organized for guests both arriving and departing. (Having guests waiting for their cars and lost tickets is not a good way to end the night!) Before your wedding thoroughly discuss your wedding timeline with your head of valet service, and make sure the company is reputable. The day of, have a point of contact (a wedding or venue coordinator) designated to keep an eye on the valets and ensure that things are running smoothly. For valet service, one of my favorite things to do is to have guests enter their car and find a favor (like a red rose or a sweet treat) inside with a thank-you note from the bride and groom.

I DO's for Transportation

- If you are getting married in prom or graduation season (April–June), when limos are in high demand, book your limo transportation in January to ensure that you won't run into a problem later on.
- Provide transportation for out-of-town guests. You can have a party bus pick up your relatives and friends from one destination to ensure that everyone gets to and from the wedding safely and without getting lost.

- Check and see if your transportation company offers a special wedding-day package that includes free champagne, favorite CD or movie, etc.
- Have your transportation arrive at least thirty minutes before the scheduled pickup in case of unexpected traffic or bad weather conditions.
- Always try to hire a company that is based in the surrounding neighborhood of your wedding, so that drivers are familiar with the area and more likely to be punctual.
- Request pictures of the exact vehicles that will be used for your big day, if you cannot go yourself to inspect them.

I DON'Ts for Transportation

- Don't hire any transportation company without getting everything in writing. Make sure that all contracts are signed by the appropriate parties. It will be one less thing you have to worry about on your wedding day.
- If you and your groom are traveling to the wedding with your bridal party, don't forget about transportation for your ladies and gents on the way home. If you arrive at the ceremony with your bridesmaids/groomsmen, you will most likely depart with your new wife/husband. Make sure that there is another vehicle to transport the bridal party to the reception and then home at the end of the night.

CHECKING IT TWICE

With all these details planned, a week before the wedding you should check in with each and every vendor, reiterating what is in your contract and what you will be receiving, as well as the timeline. Crossing your "t's" and dotting your "i's" is extremely important—vendors can be apt to forget some details. Your wedding is one of many they will do, but it is the only one they do with you, so don't feel like you are second-guessing their professionalism by double-checking that everyone is of the same mind and moving in the same direction. Take some time to make sure that everything matches up in your timeline, and gather and organize all the contact information you need. Educate and prepare your points of contact, hostesses, bridal party, and all people involved in helping you administrate the logistics of your day. Discuss with them their responsibilities, answer all their questions, and give them as much information as you have and prepare them to take over for you. Do all your trial runs, your fittings, your food sampling, your printed materials proofing, your decor approving, and any and all detailing—this is the time to tie up any loose ends and make sure that your wedding is ready to go.

Take a look at my planning chart below and make sure that everything is triumphantly checked off! Once you are comfortable, certain, and happy—kick back, relax, and get ready and focused to be the new Mrs. You!

PLANNING TIMELINE

Nine or more months ahead

- ☐ Think about the type of wedding you want—formal or informal, big or small—and the time of the year you want it to take place.
- ☐ Create budget.
- ☐ Compile guest list, and organize addresses.
- ☐ Hire wedding coordinator, if desired.
- ☐ Finalize wedding date.
- ☐ Reserve ceremony and reception sites.
- ☐ Choose attendants.
- ☐ Order dress and accessories, including veil and shoes.
- ☐ Book caterer.
- ☐ Book florist.
- ☐ Book music for ceremony and reception.
- ☐ Book photographer and videographer.
- ☐ Plan and book honeymoon.

Five to seven months ahead

- ☐ Order wedding cake.
- ☐ Send save-the-date cards, if using.
- ☐ Book officiant.
- ☐ Arrange transportation for the wedding day.
- ☐ Order stationery, including invitations and thank-you notes (earlier if designing custom pieces); book calligrapher, if using.
- ☐ Register for gifts.
- ☐ Purchase wedding rings.
- ☐ Purchase or reserve groom's attire.
- ☐ Choose attendants' attire.
- ☐ Book hotel room for wedding night.
- ☐ Reserve accommodations for out-of-town guests.
- ☐ Book hairstylist and makeup artist.

Three to five months ahead

- ☐ Reserve rental equipment, such as tables, chairs, and tents.
- ☐ Choose favors.
- ☐ Choose gifts for wedding party.
- ☐ Sign up for dance lessons, if desired.
- ☐ Discuss details of menu with caterer.
- ☐ Schedule rehearsal time and rehearsal dinner.
- ☐ Mail invitations.
- ☐ Have first dress fitting.

One to two months ahead

- ☐ Discuss service with officiant.
- ☐ Choose readings for ceremony.
- ☐ Write wedding vows, if desired.
- ☐ Have programs printed.
- ☐ Obtain marriage license, and request certified copies.
- ☐ Try out hairstyle and makeup, with veil and accessories.

☐ Contact local newspapers about publishing wedding announcement.

☐ Buy guest book.

Two weeks ahead

☐ Have final dress fitting with accessories and lingerie.

☐ Begin seating plan, and write place cards.

☐ Notify caterer of guest count.

☐ Write toasts for rehearsal dinner and wedding reception.

☐ Confirm where guests will be staying, if you plan to deliver welcome notes or gifts to their rooms.

One week ahead

☐ Finalize seating plan.

☐ Assign specific responsibilities, such as handing out corsages and boutonnieres, to members of wedding party.

☐ Pick up dress or have it delivered.

☐ Confirm details with caterer.

☐ Confirm honeymoon arrangements.

☐ Pack for honeymoon.

☐ Update caterer with final guest and vendor meal counts.

One day ahead

☐ Confirm transportation arrangements for ceremony and reception.

☐ Have manicure and pedicure.

☐ Rehearse ceremony.

☐ Hold rehearsal dinner; give gifts to wedding party.

☐ Prepare tip and payment envelopes.

Your wedding day

☐ Be a guest at your own wedding!

Twelve

THE MAIN EVENT: CEREMONY AND RECEPTION

Your ceremony is the most important part of the entire wedding: the reason all of your guests are there to see you profess your love for one another, to solidify your bond and officially become husband and wife—no longer bride and groom! *This* is the moment and the singular reason everyone has come from near and far to surround you with all their love. My reason for starting with that sentiment is to help you understand that this part of the planning is where you should spend most of your time discovering and figuring out what is unique and special to the two of you and your love, and how to make your ceremony yours and only yours. The ceremony should be overloaded with the essence of you and your husband-to-be, from your service, to your music, to all your special touches . . . everything.

You begin making the ceremony your own in the selection of the venue: a church you grew up in, your family synagogue or temple, a tent in your parent's backyard. . . . Perhaps you are a nontraditional couple, and the venue that depicts who you are might be a boat, the beach, or a great museum. As unique as ceremony venues—as well as the ceremony structure or the religion or culture that molds the ceremony—can be, they are universally the same in one very interesting aspect: The bride and groom stand next to each other, in unity. In the same way, as special as each couple is, the information I'm about to impart to you can go anywhere you go, with any ceremony and any background.

I believe that with the ceremony, understated and elegant is the way to go! I'd never say no to something creative and crazy, but candles in a church or temple can be a beautiful and romantic setting, and when it comes to your service, all you need is . . . love.

PLACES, EVERYONE!

Getting everyone ready for the show is a big part of not only being organized and calm but *appearing* organized and calm in front of your guests. This is where your planner or point of contact steps in to get your bridal party assembled, so all you must do is show up (what a life!). So from the very start, who is where and when?

The bride: In her mode of transportation (e.g., the bride stays in the car, usually with her father, who will walk her down the aisle, until the last moment). No one is to see her (especially the groom).

The groom: Tucked away from view.

Tutera Tip: None of the bridal party (including the groom) should greet anyone; in fact, none of them should be seen by the guests before the ceremony. (It's called drama!) It's like the curtain is about to go up for your performance: You, the leading lady, are not to be seen; the wedding "cast" is finally about to be revealed; and when the doors open and you are standing there, ready to walk the aisle, it's showtime!

Three Processional Orders of the Bridal Party

Traditional

The mothers of the bride and groom are seated right before the start of the processional music, after all guests are seated. (They are usually escorted by a brother of the bride or groom, or by another usher.)

After they are seated, the officiant, groom, and best man enter by a side door and wait at the altar.

Groomsmen may also enter by a side door, or can escort the bridesmaids down the aisle during the processional.

The procession order is as follows:

- Bridesmaids (with groomsmen, if desired)
- Ring Bearer and/or Flower Girl
- Maid or Matron of Honor
- Bride, escorted by her father or other close male family member or friend

Contemporary

- Officiant
- Grandparents of the groom, who are then seated in the first row
- Grandparents of the bride, who are then seated in the first row
- Groomsmen
- Best Man
- Groom, escorted by his parents
- Bridesmaids
- Maid or Matron of Honor
- Ring Bearer and/or Flower Girl
- Bride, escorted by her parents

Unconventional Variations

Some weddings (like the traditional Jewish ceremony with a chuppah) have the parents standing under the canopy with the bride and groom during the ceremony, like so:

Officiant

Bride	Groom
Parents of the Bride	Parents of the Groom
Maid or Matron of Honor	Best Man
Bridesmaids	Groomsmen

OTHER VARIATIONS INCLUDE

* The mother and father (instead of just the father) walk the bride down the aisle to give the bride away to the groom together.
* The mother and father walk halfway down the aisle, where they meet the groom, who then walks the bride the remainder of the way to the altar.
* If your mother or father can't be there to give you away, you may choose whoever is extremely important to you to fulfill this special role on their behalf: an uncle, brother, or even a significant woman in your life—what's important is that there is someone there who loves you who is honored to give you away and who supports you and your marriage.

In all cases, the bride traditionally stands on the left, and the groom on the right. This dates back to medieval times, when the groom might need to defend his bride in the middle of the ceremony, and wanted to leave his right hand free should he need to draw his sword.

Special But Not Processional

There are always special jobs for people who are able and willing to take on responsibilities! A good friend can hand out programs as the "hostess" or help guests understand which seat to sit in or where to go after the ceremony.

Gentlemen who aren't in the processional can take on the role of ushers, greeting the female guests and escorting them down the aisle to their seats before the ceremony begins. After seating each woman, the ushers are to return to the door to continue to greet and seat.

Those who aren't in the processional may have a reserved place close to the front: grandparents, readers, close family members . . . people you hand select as most important to you as bride and groom! Cordon off these areas to guarantee no confusion and instruct your ushers (and your VIPs) about these special arrangements ahead of time.

GREETING AND SEATING

If you've ever arrived at a wedding and not known which side to sit on, where to go, what rows were available and which were not, and other impending questions of life, you know *exactly* what we're trying to avoid with your wedding seating. First, no guest should ever arrive without an usher or hostess to greet and seat them.

There *is* a method to the seating madness! Your ushers can seat guests from the front rows to the back, filling in each row as they go along. Have them take special care of elders: If you know you have elders with hearing loss or guests who are disabled, have your ushers seat them with this in mind.

Reflecting how the bride and groom are standing as they face the officiant, the guests can be seated on their respective sides: guests of the bride on the left, guests of the groom on the right. (This is traditional but old world, and is not as necessary as it used to be.)

Officiant

Bride   Groom

Maid or Matron of Honor   Best Man

Bridesmaids   Groomsmen

Guests on Bridal Side: Guests on Groom Side:

Grandparents/Parents   Parents/Grandparents

Family   Family

General Guest Seating   General Guest Seating

How to Handle Late Arrivals

The old adage "better late than never" doesn't apply to entering a wedding ceremony already in progress! Your ushers should be seated in the back of the church in the close proximity to the door (or have a person stand outside at the door at all times). Instruct them to "hold" guests who come late after the processional has already started. This is also a fine role to give to your wedding coordinator. Just like a theatrical show, latecomers should wait to be seated during a break or segue in the ceremony (*not* during the middle of a song, prayer, or reading and *never ever* during the vows). If this means that they have to stand discreetly in the back or in the vestibule or foyer, then that's that—the opening and closing of doors is distracting to your congregation and, most of all, to your officiant, musicians, and you and your groom.

DETAILS, DETAILS

Programs. Have your hostess take care of your programs, either by placing them on the seats, by placing a basket holding them within reach, or by personally handing them out.

Music. Your ceremony doors should be opened to guests thirty minutes before the actual start time that was listed on your invitation. Music should be playing at all times to set the scene: Choose something romantic, calming, and beautiful—just like you!

The Runner. Before the processional starts, have someone (not you!) either preset your runner in the setup, or roll it down the aisle after the guests arrive. If you have a custom or pretty runner, it should be preset and pinned for—literally—no slipups! If it is a simple runner and you want to make a big statement (or if you need to use the center aisle for guests to get to their seats), have the runner rolled down after your guests enter and right before the processional begins.

Roping the Aisle. Once the aisle runner is down, have someone rope off the top of the aisle (the entrance end) to avoid people walking on top of the clean runner. The only people walking down the aisle runner itself should be those in the processional when the ceremony begins. Use a flower garland, a pretty ribbon, or an elegant tasseled roping. If you choose to sanction off your center aisle, make sure you have side aisles your guests can use to find their seats. The roping gets removed right before the processional starts, then your bridal party makes their way down the aisle and then . . . there you are.

HERE COMES THE BRIDE: PROCESSIONAL

There aren't many moments like the one in which you appear at the top of an aisle and then descend down it to marry your one true love. In fact, I'll rephrase that—there aren't *any* others like it in your life, at all! So take a deep breath, walk slowly, look forward at your groom, and relish every moment that is your walk toward the everlasting happiness you've waited for your whole life. When you reach the bottom of the aisle, your officiant will ask you to join hands with your groom, and will welcome your congregation.

MASTERING CEREMONY

To get the ideas flowing, I like to tell my brides and grooms to come up with five things that will make their wedding ceremony uniquely theirs and as different from the next ceremony as possible. When they look back on their wedding day, I want them to have memories of a personal, intimate, and special service that was handcrafted by themselves, for themselves.

Many begin with style, decor, and music, all perfect ways to deviate from the norm—but what really starts to shape the *content* of the ceremony is what I (and your guests) find interesting.

Delve into traditions inspired by everything from family to religion to culture and folklore. Traditions mainly vary depending on religion (from a Catholic Mass, Greek Orthodox ceremony, or Baptist service to a Jewish or Indian service, the many symbolisms and practices that help define the bride and groom are endless!). There are so many formalities based on your culture that it becomes a very personal choice to decide how religious (or not) or how serious (or not) you want your ceremony and service to be. Heritage and religion actually play a larger role in setting the pace and the happenings in your ceremony, so I find it's the perfect place to begin molding your service. Use the structure of your cultural or religious traditions, and then build additional personal touches of your own into it.

The ceremony concepts in this chapter are designed to be able to be universally dropped into any kind of ceremony, with any formalities or customs that are important to you!

Music is such a strong way to tell your story. Have someone—either someone you know, someone from your place of worship or from your entertainment vendor, or someone you hire—vocalize a piece that moves you, and that has meaning to you and your groom. When selecting the right piece of music, ask yourself how you can musically share who you are with your guests.

The bride and groom can each pick someone special in their lives (it could be someone near and dear, old or young, or in or out of the bridal party) and ask them to speak to your guests on a one-word topic: love.

Have both individuals speak for three to five minutes; it's a short but touching and simple way to make your service that much more unique and that much more special to you. Give your speakers guidelines: Tell them this is a speech on love, objectively—not a religious reading and also not a toast to you and your groom (that means no "When I first met these two . . ." stories!). The speaker should focus on making his or her words more like a sharing, or a proclamation to why everyone is gathered there: It's a moving sentiment that brings everyone back to the fundamental meaning and feeling of love.

In addition to exchanging rings, choose a special wedding "tradition" that you and your groom will complete. Light a unity candle, jump the broom, break the glass, pour two separate colors of sand into one bottle, release doves, or observe your union with a ritual of cultural significance. This act will contribute to telling the story of you, now and in the future when you remember your wedding day.

Tutera Tip: For destination weddings on the beach, I love the concept of pouring sand together to symbolize your union. From two separate glass containers, each filled with different-colored sand (one for the bride and one for the groom), the bride and the groom then pour their sand into one, a perfect blend that can never be separated.

Tutera Tip: The bride always walks down the aisle on the left side of her father/escort. An easy way to remember is this: A little girl is always "close to her father's heart"!

DO YOU TAKE THIS MAN?: VOWS

It's a wonderful idea for the bride and groom to write their own wedding vows. The ceremony is the perfect time to share your heartfelt thoughts with each other. Telling a short story of how you met or when you knew you were in love can make the most special of days even more so for you. Remember, the ceremony is the time that truly belongs to you, and only you, as a couple. Your vows are a verbal celebration of your love and commitment to one another! It may be challenging to put such emotion into words and into an everlasting promise, but it's well worth it—ask for help from friends and loved ones, borrow words of poets, or write from the heart. At the end of the day (and at the start of your life), it's just nice to hear the bride and groom as who they truly are. The groom speaks first, followed by the bride. Make sure you, your groom, and your officiant are all sound amplified so everyone can hear you!

Tutera Tip: On your first anniversary, have your vows framed and give them as a gift to each other.

MAKE IT OFFICIAL: HIRING AN OFFICIANT

Oh, how many Hail Marys I said when I watched one bride's (thankfully not one of my clients) pastor mispronounce her name the entire ceremony. The officiant of your wedding should be someone who knows you and your groom, who understands who you are as a couple . . . someone who should rightfully be solidifying you into a serious union. No rent-a-rabbi or purchase-a-priest. You have to find someone, whether it's through going to a church and seeking out the officiant, asking a friend, or searching for one on the Internet. Don't introduce yourself to your officiant for the first time when you walk down the aisle! You have to meet the person and have a connection with him or her. The officiant has to know something about you: how and where you fell in love, what makes you two perfect for one another, why you are going to be something special. Meet with him or her. (The sad truth: Some brides spend more time with their cake baker than with their officiant, so don't let that hold true for you!)

When deciding if an officiant is the right fit for you, describe to him or her what kind of ceremony you are looking for, see what he or she typically provides, and hopefully, you will make a match!

Tutera Tip: *You likely do not want a same-old, same-old wedding service that can be repeated for everyone and anyone! A wedding service can be just the opposite, tailored to you and created specifically for you and your groom. When you step into a house of worship, your limitations are greater (because of the need to abide by tradition and service structure), but search for ways you can make your ceremony unique to you, unlike any other ceremony your guests have seen and will see.*

Tutera Tip: *Make sure all your marriage licenses and legal and religious paperwork is handled before you get married! Forgetting these documents happens too often and can delay your ceremony!*

THERE GOES THE BRIDE: RECESSIONAL

The first down the aisle toward the exit are you, the bride and groom. Exit with the grace you came in with (i.e., please do not fist pump the air, or whirl the bouquet around your head and yell "whooo" or any other kind of indecipherable noise of jubilance). Walk down the aisle, be poised, and show your joy in a great smile!

Your bridal party should follow, filtering out in reverse order from the processional.

At that point, have your bridal party form the receiving line at the exit and start your thank-yous!

TO GIVE IS TO RECEIVE: RECEIVING LINES

Receiving lines are the formal, traditional way to thank your guests for attending, and they also allow guests the opportunity to offer their congratulations to the newlyweds. Each and every guest has made arrangements and shown value in seeing you get married, so please take a moment to greet them (with so many people and such a busy night ahead of you, this may be the only time you are able to see some of them!). In a receiving line, you can estimate that it will take thirty minutes to greet a hundred guests. Should time not allow for a receiving line, make sure that you greet each table during your reception, but if you can manage to fit one in after your ceremony or before your reception, it is a wonderful touch. The receiving line is the perfect place to meet certain guests on your spouse's side for the first time; it's lovely to start your marriage together with greetings.

The order of your receiving line should be:

- Bride
- Groom
- Mother of the Bride
- Father of the Bride
- Mother of the Groom
- Father of the Groom

Tutera Tip: The host family (read: whoever is paying) lines up first after the bride and groom. Example: If the groom's family is paying, it would be the bride and groom followed by the groom's family, then the bride's.

After the bride and the groom and the parents, you may opt to keep it simple with just these six people, but if you choose to continue on, the next in line are:

- Maid or Matron of Honor
- Best Man

You may stop here, or continue with the formal (and longest) way by then including:

- All the bridesmaids
- All the groomsmen

If you have a large bridal party, I suggest leaving it to just the parents and possibly the maid or matron of honor and the best man (if they know a good number of people on the guest list, they can help guests feel welcome and extend thanks on your behalf). Too much hand-shaking and introductions can be overwhelming to both your bridal attendants and your guests, so in the case of receiving lines, formal and traditional is not always best. The key to a successful receiving line is short, sweet, and sincere.

I DO'S for Receiving Lines
- When greeting, always make eye contact with your guests to avoid creating an assembly-line feel. It makes it so much more personal.
- Keep things very sincere and short so you're not spending too much time with one person over the next. Always keep people moving along (there are many others waiting in line behind them!). Speak with your receiving-line "team" about how to handle people who talk too long—one of your "next in lines" can help move the conversation down the line.

I DON'Ts for Receiving Lines
- If there is a guest or someone you haven't seen in years, extend gratefulness, but never make them feel uncomfortable or as if you don't remember them!

- Don't look over your guest's shoulder to see who is next in line or what else may be happening in the room. Always seem engaged in the people you are greeting.

When you're finished greeting your guests and it's your time to exit for your transportation (and off to the reception you go), it's customary for your guests to shower you with luck on your way out. Throwing rice (for fertility) at wedding ceremonies is no longer common practice or even allowed in some cases, but guests should have fun when the happy couple walks by after the ceremony. In recent years, more modern toss options have included:

- Flower petals
- Birdseed (very earth-friendly)
- Lavender buds
- Bubbles
- Confetti
- Doves
- Butterfly releases—also great to happen on the words "I do" (outdoors only)

Tutera Tip: Check to see what your location allows in regard to toss items.

- Upon your exit, special music can also be a great send-off (and perhaps a great surprise wedding present for you or your groom!). One of my grooms surprised his bride with a choir singing "Ode to Joy," and one of my brides surprised her groom with a Spanish guitarist, a nod to his heritage. Herald trumpets playing outside the church is also great fanfare.
- As you get into your mode of transportation to head off to the reception, just make sure someone (bridal party member, hostess, mom-in-law, etc.) is there to help your guests know where they are going so all can easily join you for the party!

CELEBRATE GOOD TIMES: YOUR COCKTAILS AND RECEPTION

If your ceremony was your debut, your cocktail hour serves as an intermission, and it's only fitting that your reception is your "second act"! Don't fall into the trap of thinking that you were only "onstage" for the ceremony when everyone was seated and all eyes were on you—your stardom continues all through the night, and in the same way you had to script out the first act, a lot of planning and preparation needs to go into bringing down the house for the remainder of the show, so when the curtain finally goes up, you can relax and be in all your center-stage glory.

When it comes to your reception, it's all about the flow and the precision of execution. This is where you must rely on the catering manager, the on-site coordinator, or your point person and just take a deep breath—from this moment forward, let it all go and enjoy yourself and your hard work! (No bride of mine will be jumping out of her seat to cue the band or run the show!) If you trusted the right people, chose the right vendors, and did all the right planning, this moment is where this book means the most to you. It's where all your months of planning and being detail-obsessed pays off, where you can sit and relax and be a guest at your own wedding.

To make sure you have that moment of bliss at your reception, confirm that every single vendor has a copy of your timeline. Everyone, at all times, has to be on the same page, know what you expect, and be prepared to move the party along and do their role. (The reception is where a well-executed wedding is a well-executed wedding, and a chaotic wedding is a chaotic wedding! There is no happy medium.)

The cocktail hour is the first time when everybody is together in one space. Where people can mingle, greet, and so on before you enter into your reception celebration. "Cocktails" is where new people are meeting, the other sides of the family are greeting each other, old friends and family are seeing one another again for the first time in ages, etc. After an hour's time, everyone should have arrived to the venue and should be ready for the fun to really begin!

AND NOW . . . THE ANNOUNCEMENT OF THE BRIDAL PARTY

Let's party! The revealing of the reception room is one of my favorite parts of the wedding. It's like unveiling a world of wonder, where guests trickle in and each exclaims delight with what they see. When you start your reception, have a grand opening of the doors and strike up the band right as they open. Let your waitstaff or banquet captains go group to group to invite your guests to be seated for dinner if people are slow to leave the cocktail area.

Once your guests have seen the room, have found their seats, and have settled in, the bridal party should enter. This is usually fifteen minutes or so after the opening of the doors. Have the DJ or the bandleader make an announcement that either the bridal party or the bride and groom will be entering (this will cue everyone to be seated, including anyone who rushed straight to the dance floor and could simply not wait to start cutting a rug).

Before your wedding, discuss with the bandleader the way in which you want your bridal party to be announced. Three options (the second of which is my favorite):

1. Only the announcement of the bride and groom as husband and wife
2. No announcement of the bridal party
3. Everyone from the processional at the ceremony is reintroduced into the room

Tutera Tip: I have mentioned this before, but it's worth saying twice: Make sure your announcer can pronounce each and everyone's names correctly. Give them a phonetic list of how each name sounds.

When you and your groom are announced, enter together, holding hands, and instead of doing an egregious jump or running around the room giving out high fives, I would like to suggest you come in and either wave, kiss each other, or even have him spin you around and do a dip. If you choose to do your first dance right away, head straight to the dance floor and have your music begin promptly.

MAY I HAVE THIS DANCE?: SPECIAL DANCES

When I ask brides what moments are high on their importance list, the father/daughter dance is always, always close behind the vow exchange. I find this priority trend so endearing because, ladies, the father/daughter dance is high up on your dad's *life* importance list. Your three dances (bride and groom, father/daughter, and mother/son) are three of life's most special moments for all six of the people involved and are guaranteed to make hearts melt and tears fall. Whether they are your father's, your own, sappy Uncle Jim's, your guests, or all of the above, your special dances are sentimental for all. In order, with song suggestions, the dances are:

1. Bride and Groom
   - "L-O-V-E"—Frank Sinatra
   - "You're the First, the Last, My Everything"—Barry White
   - "It Had to Be You"—Harry Connick, Jr.
   - "When I Fall in Love"—Natalie Cole and Nat King Cole
   - "You Are So Beautiful"—Joe Cocker
   - "Just the Way You Are"—Billy Joel

- "It's Your Love"—Tim McGraw and Faith Hill
- "Amazed"—Lonestar
- "I Could Not Ask for More"—Edwin McCain
- "When I Say I Do"—Clint Black and Lisa Hartman Black
- "I Swear"—All-4-One
- "I Finally Found Someone"—Barbra Streisand
- "I Do (Cherish You)"—98 Degrees/Mark Wills
- "Endless Love"—Lionel Richie and Diana Ross
- "Breathe"—Faith Hill
- "All the Way"—Celine Dion and Frank Sinatra
- "True"—Ryan Cabrera

2. Father and Daughter

- "Butterfly Kisses"—Bob Carlisle
- "Brown Eyed Girl"—Van Morrison
- "My Father's Eyes"—Eric Clapton
- "Sweet Child o' Mine"—Sheryl Crow
- "Dance with My Father"—Luther Vandross
- "Father and Daughter"—Paul Simon
- "Daughters"—John Mayer
- "God Only Knows"—The Beach Boys
- "The Way You Look Tonight"—Tony Bennett
- "Fly Me to the Moon"—Frank Sinatra
- "Because You Loved Me"—Celine Dion
- "Angel"—Sarah McLachlan
- "Lullabye"—Billy Joel
- "Thank Heaven for Little Girls"—Maurice Chevalier
- "I Loved Her First"—Heartland
- "There You'll Be"—Faith Hill
- "Through the Years"—Kenny Rogers
- "Sunshine of My Life"—Stevie Wonder
- "I'll Stand By You"—The Pretenders
- "Wonderful Tonight"—Eric Clapton
- "Unforgettable"—Natalie Cole

- "You Got It"—Roy Orbison
- "My Girl"—The Temptations

3. Mother and Son
- "In My Life"—The Beatles
- "Wind Beneath My Wings"—Bette Midler
- "A Song for Mama"—Boyz II Men
- "Isn't She Lovely"—Stevie Wonder
- "Somewhere Over the Rainbow"—Israel Kamakawino'ole
- "What a Wonderful World"—Louis Armstrong
- "I Hope You Dance"—Lee Ann Womack
- "My Wish"—Rascal Flatts
- "Have I Told You Lately"—Rod Stewart
- "Beautiful in My Eyes"—Joshua Kadison
- "Forever Young"—Alphaville
- "Blessed"—Elton John
- "You're the Inspiration"—Chicago
- "I Turn to You"—Christina Aguilera

I DO's for Entering the Reception and First Dances
- Choreograph your dances! Take dance classes with your groom, your father, or both! Dance classes are great for a variety of reasons: They allow the bride and groom to feel comfortable on the dance floor, a good dance is less awkward for the guests to watch from the sidelines, and classes are a great stress buster during the planning process. You can always use dancing skills for the rest of your life.
- Make sure that everyone is present when they need to be. It's the worst when the DJ or bandleader announces, "Please join us on the dance floor as the father/daughter dance takes place," and the father is nowhere to be found! He's at the bar, he's in the restroom, he's somewhere crying about how his baby daughter is all grown up. . . . No place other

than the dance floor is appropriate when this announcement is made. The DJ or bandleader has to have a point person to make sure that his announcements are timed well.

- Have your maid/matron of honor nearby with tissues for any weepy moments anyone participating in your special dances may have!

I DON'Ts for Entering the Reception and First Dances

- Such a classy bride (I'm talking about you!) should never be accompanied by cheesy music! As you enter as bride and groom . . . please just say no to "Eye of the Tiger," the theme from the movie *Rocky*, or any rendition of something even *close* to "I'm Too Sexy." Think of your announced entrance just as seriously as if you were selecting music to accompany you as you accept an Oscar. The Academy announced your name, you're coming down to the stage, you're the center of attention, you're wearing a great gown, you're glowing with excitement, and your song is . . . (Hopefully you just thought of a great song and not something that would play if you were about to jump in a wrestling ring.)
- Don't dance the whole song through. Do sixty to ninety seconds, then fade it out or ask other people to join you. There's nothing worse than a too-long dance to strain the mood. Have you ever watched a bride and groom rock back and forth awkwardly and been bored out of your mind for four minutes of "(Everything I Do) I Do It For You"? Please don't let this be you. Your first dance should be a crowd-pleasing, smashing success!

Following special dances, make sure you are smiling your happiest smile and, with your groom, make your way to your seats at your sweetheart table. In this first portion of your reception, you should take a moment to dine with your groom, eat something, listen to toasts given to you, and mingle a bit.

The order of your reception events (your special dances and your toasts) is entirely up to you—my only request is that you space out each occurrence throughout the party to avoid back-to-back interruptions and keep a constant flow of music. Usually, though, your first toasts from the party hosts should happen early as a welcome to your guests.

CHEERS!: TOASTS GIVEN ON YOUR SPECIAL DAY

Giving a toast honors many things: you and your groom, your wedding day itself, and the person giving the toast. All components make toasts some of the most important moments in your special day. A heartfelt sentiment from a loved one, be it a best friend or a parent, can move the emotions of an entire room and even bring tears of joy.

It's said that toasting originates from ancient times, when sacrifices of luxurious wines were offered to gods and goddesses in return for longevity of life and good health. I offer this section of toasting etiquette to you, to honor your long life together with your groom, and to your health!

Cheers!

I DO's for Proper Toasting

- Follow the proper order of toast giving. The first toast is by the father of the bride. If the parents are still married, they should be side by side all night (or especially during the toasts). Separate the following toasts—avoid doing one after another, after another; there will be no speech-giving marathons! Choose different points in the evening's timeline to designate when each toast should be given. (This also plays to the "something different every thirty minutes" rule!)

- The second toast should be given by the groom's parents. This is not a necessity (it only becomes mandatory if they are paying for the wedding, in which whoever is paying would go first), but it can be welcomed if you'd like to include them in the moment.

- The third toasts are shared between the best man and the maid or matron of honor. Last, I personally believe a bride and groom should give a toast to everyone who is there. This is the perfect opportunity to thank their parents, their friends and family, and all the guests for traveling here. This is also an appropriate time to pay tribute to the memory of people who have passed on and people who could not be there. The bride and groom should go last.

- Do let your toasters know how you'd like them to prepare. For toasts, short and sweet is the name of the game. Politely ask your "toasters" to keep it short and sans embarrassing moments and private jokes that leave your guests out or would require a long explanation! (And this is not a roast!) I always say if you want to start adding other toasts, remember each one is taking your time away from celebrating your day. Leave your guests wanting more, not wishing your best man would take another swig and just fall over already.

- Select special toasting flutes for you and your groom to use at your wedding. These two special glasses will be with you forever, to celebrate special occasions with and to remember the day you married and all the warm wishes that you received with them. Bring them out on your anniversary each year and on special moments to continue to toast to your prosperity well after your wedding day.

I DON'Ts for Proper Toasting

- Don't have a marathon of speeches! If you'd like your bridesmaids, groomsmen, ushers, or other important family members to say a few words, invite them to do so at the rehearsal dinner (rather than at the wedding). Give them time limitations and if they have trouble finding a topic, ask them to speak about love or to tell a short story about you as a couple.

- Don't be caught empty-handed! Make sure you and your groom have a filled glass of something sparkly for each toast. The person toasting you should also follow suit. Assign one of your bridesmaids the task of ensuring that a caterer takes care of topping off those who are involved with the toasting. When toasting and sipping, hold your glass by the stem, and not by the bell (the part that holds the liquid). At the culmination of each toast, raise your glass and clink gently. When you are giving or receiving a toast, always look into the eyes of the other person and make a connection with them as you share or hear words.

Tutera Tip: Speaking of libations . . . just as in the reception line, have someone looking out for you. Either your groom or someone in your bridal party should be your "bodyguard" against guests who have been enjoying the beverages a little too much! The last thing you need is to be cornered by your long-lost cousin who may try to talk your ear off or tell you unending stories of your (or worse, their) youth. One fifteen-minute charity conversation is fifteen minutes you could have spent dancing with your groom (and tipsy individuals may not even remember your sacrifice!). Have a few lines prepared: "My mother is looking for me!" or "I have to check in with the band!" or "Did I just see someone stick a finger into the cake? Please excuse me" will do just fine.

LET THE GAMES BEGIN!:
CAKE, GARTER, BOUQUET

The cake-cutting, the garter toss, and the bouquet toss: the three essential acts that no guest leaves without seeing! My feelings about each of these is very much the same across the board: They should be as classy, quick, and sweet as possible, paying homage to tradition without interrupting the flow of your party.

The right timing for these is (a) all at once, and (b) after the entrée is cleared and right before a very high-energy song that gets everyone up and moving! A simple announcement by your DJ or bandleader will do the trick to get everyone ready—don't let your announcer grab the microphone and go on and on, and most important, don't stop the music (always have something on in the background; there should never be dead silences at any point during these moments!). It's important to have all three events happen at once. Any time you divert the party flow, it brings the party to a dead halt, so have your DJ or band line up a dance favorite ready to be played as soon as the toss is over to bring the party swing back into motion!

It's a Cake Walk

The cutting of the cake should be prominent, an event itself. Your wedding cake should be front and center from the beginning—it's a great aesthetic and should be a big deal visually, and be lit if possible. You spent so much time picking it out and paying for it, it deserves to be on display! Have your caterer or one of your bridal attendants be queued with the cake-cutting flatware and get ready to make a wish!

Lingerie: Tossing the Garter

I have to admit, I'm very anti–garter toss. I wish I could tell you not to do it—it's very easy for me to tell a bride that this "tradition" actually has no place in a classy party, but to have her actually listen is another story. So if you're going to do it—make it quick! Make it simple! Please do not play the *Jeopardy!* theme song or handcuff anyone or make small children watch (or worse, participate . . .). All I ask is that you just think about how you're going to do it (it's pretty awkward for everyone to watch the groom reach up the bride's skirt, not to mention unfair to then measure her luck in inches . . . really!). Put the garter on low, have your groom easily retrieve it without being swallowed by your dress, and call it a day! Phew! Do it, be done with it, and crank up the music!

The Windup and the Pitch: The Bouquet Toss

Now, tossing the bouquet I love. This tradition dates back to the medieval times, where a bride's guests used to actually claw at her dress as she walked down the aisle to get a bit of her luck in love (how's that for sharing the love!). It then evolved into the bride tossing a smaller bouquet to the single women to pass on the luck . . . much better than ripping the gorgeous white gown to shreds!

This can happen right after the garter toss and cake-cutting, but I love to see this happen at the end, as the bride is leaving the reception in her "going away outfit." Think the timing at the end of the movie *My Best Friend's Wedding*: Cameron Diaz, dressed in a fabulous white going away outfit, throws the bouquet to Julia Roberts on her way out the door as her guests bid her farewell, and then drives off in a vintage car with Dermot Mulroney. *That's* how it's done!

The point is to pass on the luck, and there's no better time to do that than with your sweet farewell at the end of the night!

FAVORITE FAVORS

Kids say the darndest things, and any preadolescent at a birthday party will tell you how excited they are to get the goodie bag. Yes, we have much to gather from our society's youth: Kids of all ages like to get surprise treats at a party, and somewhere inside even the most mature adult, good wedding favors will elicit that same response. We may not be running around the party hopped up on candy, playing with fake jewelry and toy airplanes, but a well-chosen favor (read: not just your average box of mints-in-a-tin) will provoke the grown-up version of that: surprise, delight, and appreciation of your kind gesture.

It pains me when a bride and groom spend money on a favor that is destined to be tossed aside because of lack of practicality, quality, or—simply put—good taste. The right favors don't have to be expensive by any means; they just need to be selected tastefully, presented properly, and coordinated with the overall picture of your wedding (tie them in to your colors, your wedding style, your venue or location, or your time of the year). Your wedding favors aren't just trinkets to give your guests because of the obligation of wedding protocol. Your wedding favors are your last opportunities to wrap up the "wedding story" you've been telling all along. To me, they are the beautifully scripted "The End" at the end of a fairy tale. It's just not complete without them (and they need to be beautifully done for the full effect).

UNIQUE FUN FAVOR IDEAS
- S'mores and marshmallow skewers
- Luggage tags
- Candy apples
- Fans (for beach wedding)
- Nice chopsticks tied with pretty ribbon (for Asian theme)
- Flip-flops
- Scented candles that match the style/season of wedding
- Hand-blown glass flowers
- Compasses with the inscription "May love be your guide in life"
- Unique paperweights
- Napkin rings
- Blankets or pashmina scarves
- Bottles or splits of wine
- Photos printed by a portable printer on-site, framed

- Letter openers
- Edible chocolate menus
- Seeds or "plantable" paper with a thank-you message
- Your grandmother's favorite cookie recipe with the recipe card attached to either cookies or dry ingredients
- Jars full of a variety of candy in your wedding colors, with a candy refill station on the way out
- Herbs in small galvanized pots (for outdoor wedding)
- Wrapped soaps in the colors of your wedding
- Pretty bookmarks made of flat metal in the shape of a heart or symbol from your wedding
- Drink mixes with recipes like spiced cider, hot cocoa, or iced tea
- Elegant bottle stoppers or wine keys/openers or pourers
- Jar of jam, hot fudge sauce, honey, salsa, BBQ sauce, etc.
- Recipes and ingredients/tools to make your signature cocktail—mojito muddlers, margarita salt, a package of rimmer and swizzle sticks
- Apples in a burlap bag with an apple pie recipe
- Fun salt and pepper shakers that match your wedding style
- Instant-edit DVDs of your wedding
- CDs of music heard at the wedding

Tutera Tip: Add an expensive look to favors by making them personal and directing your money away from things like tulle and unnecessary boxing and toward chic elegant ribbons or tags. You may not even need to wrap them in fabric (why cover a great gift?). A nicely printed and designed tag with a message and your logo or monogram on it will look clean and correlating.

Tutera Tip: Speaking of take-home items, don't let flowers go to waste. Have your caterer arrange for the waitstaff to remove the flowers and wrap them in tissue with a bow for guests to take with them as they leave.

As your reception draws to a close and your greetings turn to thank-yous and good-byes, it's my hope you will be flooded with emotions of joy, relief, happiness, overwhelming love, joyous exhaustion, and unending excitement for what's to come next. As you depart with your groom, add a successful wedding and planning well done to your list of things to celebrate in your quiet moments with one another! In your postwedding reflection, know that I am proud of you and could not be happier that you made your fantasy into a reality, from ordinary into extraordinary. Say your good-byes, and off you go to your wedding night and long-awaited relaxation!

Closing

HAPPILY-EVER-AFTER-THE-WEDDING'S-OVER

My wish for you is that my *Big White Book of Weddings* will help you look back upon your wedding day with nothing but a heart full of memories of everything. . . . The way he looked when he saw you. How you felt in your dress. Your walk down the aisle. The way your bridesmaids smiled. How much you loved your bouquet. The vows you spoke. The beauty of the declarations. Dancing with your father. The toast from the best man. The sight when you walked into your reception. The band playing your favorite song. Delicious and beautiful food. Your guests laughing and enjoying themselves . . . Most important, I hope you will remember the great extent to which you enjoyed yourself the whole day through! That to me determines a successful wedding—not how perfectly everything went or how nothing unexpected came up . . . not even necessarily what everyone will say about it for years to come. There's no greater wedding gift you could give yourself than what you've been doing all along—loving, learning, and hopefully laughing along the way.

When you're through with the wedding-planning process, you will have accomplished one of your life's largest tasks, and you will have done so with your groom, for the glory of love—what a perfect start to a marriage! You've now prepared yourself for a stylish, sophisticated, graceful, polished, beautiful, poised, and good-humored life (sounds like perhaps your wedding won't be the only thing that is the best version of itself!).

I'm so thankful you allowed me to be a part of your special wedding. And don't worry—I'll be here waiting with tips on how to throw a great housewarming bash when you newlyweds settle in (and if you thought planning your wedding was fun, get ready to become a home entertainer!). Now get going! You have a honeymoon and the start of a whole fabulous new life awaiting you, so celebrate that new life together in *style*!

Index